A Mother's Journey
Grief

Valerie Jones

Dedication

To my children, who inspired me to embrace my greatness and loved me with every heartbeat. My son, you will always be my joy, and my daughter, you will always be my strength.

To all my dearest friends, family, supporters, and readers who have helped turn these pages into reality, I am deeply grateful.

Acknowledgment

Gratitude constantly plays in my heart for those who generously gave provision for the essential tools that empowered me (to get healthy) in this journey. My appreciation also extends to my support group friends and family, whose love and encouragement have been my guiding light throughout this journey.

About the Author

Valerie Jones is a dedicated activist with a long-standing commitment to social change and justice. With a background in Business, Valerie has used her education to create meaningful impacts in various communities. She loves reading and writing and enjoys helping others think creatively. Valerie tries to blend her advocacy to inspire people to look within themselves and find deeper meaning in life while staying committed to making the world a better place.

Table of Contents

Preface

Life, in its grand, messy beauty, can throw us tragedies we never imagined. Mine came in the form of losing not one but two of my most precious children. Denee, my bright and eldest, was ripped away far too soon from my life at the age of forty-one. She was a mother to two beautiful children herself and squeezed every drop of joy from life, doing things that made her happy. My youngest, Darrell, was the family jokester with a heart full of delight. He left a void in my heart that no laughter can quite fill. He valued his family and friends with a fierce loyalty.

The pain of losing both my children is a continuous hurt that sometimes flares into a sharp, searing pain. Going through my own grief, I also felt a lot of anger. There have been days, the very worst ones, where the thought of my surviving daughter and her own pain has choked me with guilt. The feeling of failing to protect any of my children, then or now, is a heavy burden.

Nonetheless, I found that gratitude is something that makes us see the brighter side of things. It may seem counterintuitive, but despite losing Denee and Darrell, I've found peace in remembering them with love. Yes, there have been moments where despair threatened to drown me, but I haven't been entirely consumed.

I would never dream of denying the absence of my children nor the way I hold dear every memory we shared. However, I'm now able to acknowledge the immense happiness, joy, and comfort they brought into my life. I am grateful for the time we had together.

While going through the throbbing pain of losing the lights of my life, I began to pour my heart out onto the paper. I started journaling and was able to write the raw, uncensored emotions I felt about the entire situation. As I wrote, I realized that countless mothers grapple with similar losses like mine, with a grief that feels all-consuming and hopeless. There's a pressure to "move on" to find a silver lining, but sometimes all we can find are tears.

This book is for those mothers. This book is for those people who are struggling to get out of a trauma but can't find the strength to get up and walk toward a brighter future. Through my story, I hope to offer a hand to hold, a voice to say, "You're not alone."

The pain does remain like a sharp pang that can catch me off guard in the most ordinary places – a grocery store aisle, a scene in a movie. But through my journey, I've come to understand that even in the middle of a storm, there can be sunshine. Healing can coexist with pain. This book is evidence of that. It's a story of loss, yes, but also of love and resilience. It's for mothers who feel lost, for anyone struggling with a grief that feels all-encompassing. It's a message of hope, a beacon in the darkness, saying: There is light to be found, even after the storm.

Chapter 1: November 7th - A Day That Changed Everything

It was a quiet Monday night, November 7th, 2022. We were all busy with our usual routines, having dinner together, and then I settled in for some TV. I clearly remember 'The Cleaning Lady' playing on the screen. My children were in the front of the house, and I was in the bedroom at the back.

Suddenly, I heard a sharp sound. Then another, and another. The fast staccato of what sounded like automatic weapons fire shook me upright. At first, I ignored and continued watching the TV, thinking it was no reason to be alarmed but when I heard the sound continuously, my heart started beating fast. I froze for a moment as the silliness of the situation briefly overrode my fear. Surely, it couldn't be gunfire. Not here, not in our quiet neighborhood.

Convincing myself it was just some loud fireworks or construction gone wrong, I hesitantly turned back to the TV. But a prickling nervousnesswas there in my heart. A little while later, a different sound reached me through the house. It was a stifled thud, like something bumping into a wall. I could hear some low murmurs. Alarm bells tolled in my head. I couldn't ignore it any longer. I wanted to know what was going on, so I tiptoed to the door as my heartbeat got faster and faster.

As I opened the door and stepped into the hallway, I found them…my children. That scene is something that is imprinted in my brain like a burnt mark. I still remember their faces…their eyes…everything.

I immediately dialed for the emergency services, and the following time, waiting for them felt like forever. It was like a cruel punishment on top of the horror I had already witnessed. When the officers finally arrived, they seemed weary and almost indifferent. They looked tired and overloaded, and it seemed like they didn't think it was that important. It took forever before they secured the scene and began their investigation. The delayed response was the biggest challenge that night.

The impersonal way they treated me only added to my already disjointed state. Here I was, my life shattered, my world turned upside down, and it felt like they viewed me as just another statistic and burden on their already stretched resources. They didn't seem to get how scared I still was or how awful everything had just been.

To put it simply, everything changed that night. I felt completely unsafe, like my own home wasn't a safe place anymore. It was messed up. Even with the repairs, it doesn't feel cozy or happy anymore. The worst part, though, is that my children aren't here. I miss their laughter, their plans for the future, everything they could have been. Their lives were taken away for no reason at all.

Looking back, I think the shock was so strong that my emotions were delayed. Maybe that's why I didn't feel the full weight of it all right away. It wasn't until that night when they told me about my son... that he had expired...that's when it hit me.

My son... was gone.

The ground seemed to rush up to meet me. I could feel the room spinning. The last thing I remember was a darkness closing in. I fainted. And since then, it's been like a wave of sadness crashing over me again and again. All the emotions of grief come rushing back, over and over. I cried a lot and found myself shedding big tears that felt heavy and never seemed to stop. I got really, really angry, like a volcano exploding. Then I felt sad and empty like everything was pointless. There was guilt that settled in my gut. Did I miss some sign? Could I have done something differently? It was a continuous battle. But I took a deep breath, and for the sake of my surviving daughter, I kept going.

But I haven't been alone in this storm. I'm so grateful

for the incredible support system that surrounded me. My neighbors, the church community, and even strangers rallied around me. They were there for me in countless ways, big and small. They helped me clean up the house, which was really hard, but having them there made it a little easier. They shouldered the burden of funeral arrangements, which allowed me some space to simply breathe and process the unimaginable.

Their financial support was also a big help during a time when even the most basic tasks felt too hard. They offered to pay bills, covered grocery costs, and helped with some of the unexpected expenses that arose in the wake of the loss. A GoFundMe page was set up, which helped tremendously. But more than the financial help, it was the shared grief, the listening ears, and the helping hands that made a world of difference.

Some friends also suggested I talk to a grief counselor, someone who could help me deal with my sadness. At first, I wasn't sure if it would help, but they were really nice about it, and I knew I needed something. Going to counseling turned out to be a really good thing for me.

My friends didn't just help with the big things; they thought of the little things, too. Lots of them sent me cards with nice messages to let me know they cared. Others offered rides to appointments when I was feeling really tired and sad. There were also other individuals who offered words of comfort, practical assistance, and prayers. Friends, family, and even strangers all helped me drive through this new normal, a life without my children. Their kindness is a debt I can never repay.

A year and a half have passed. Birthdays have come and gone; holidays uncelebrated. The pain of my children's absence feels constant. The investigation by the authorities seems to have stalled. It's frustrating to think that after all this time, there haven't been any answers.

The memory of that night is seared into my mind. Two cars pulled up with their staccato bursts of gunfire echoing through the street. With so many people around, surely someone saw something, someone remembers something. But even the silence from the streets is deafening. Eighteen months have passed, and yet the gunmen remain unidentified. I hold onto the hope that someday, someone will come forward with information.

Making sense of this pain felt almost impossible to bear. But I've learned that challenges like these, as difficult as they are, are a part of life's journey. There's a strange kind of courage that comes from accepting the hardship. It's a courage that allows me to take a deep breath, wipe away the tears, and keep putting one foot in front of the other. It's the strength to keep going, not because things are easy, but because I know that's what my children would have wanted for me. It's not about forgetting my children or minimizing the pain but about finding a way to carry it with me as I move forward.

Chapter 2: Holding Onto Love While Letting Go

Grief is a strange and detaching journey. While the world seems to be moving on with their lives, you're left standing still, trapped in the memories of what used to be. One of the biggest challenges for me has been watching family and friends celebrate milestones - the arrival of a new baby, the first wobbly steps, and all the celebrations related to children. It's like I'm stuck in a slow-motion movie, watching everyone else fast forward through their lives. The happiness they feel is genuine, of course, but it stabs a fresh twinge of pain into my heart. I miss those milestones with my own children. I also feel happy for those family and friends, but I'm only human and feel that utter sadness deep inside.

It's a tightrope walk, this balancing act of grief. On one side, there's the irresistible need to scream out my pain, to let the world know the hole my children have left in my heart. But on the other side, there's this fear of burdening others, of dulling their delight with my grief.

Nonetheless, the love I have for my children never fades. They weren't perfect, of course. No one is. They had their quirks and their moments of frustration, just like any normal human being. But that's part of what made them so precious to me.

One of my favorite memories of my son comes rushing back to me - a snapshot from when he was just three years old. We were at the grocery store, and in a moment of pure toddler mischief, he launched a small ball into one of those high, out-of-reach baskets. As I watched it bounce around, I saw a future basketball star in the making. Of course, life had other plans, and it wouldn't be wrong to say that I was utterly wrong when he ended up becoming an electrician.

Another memory of my children is from the day I brought my daughter home from the hospital. She was bundled up in a little pink and blue blanket. She was snuggled safely in my arms. My mom was driving us home that evening. I remember looking down at my daughter, feeling an irresistible sense of protectiveness, as if I was holding the most precious doll in the world.

These memories, bittersweet as they are, are a source of little light in the storm. They remind me of the immense love I shared with my children.

One of the things I miss most about my son is his way of using words. He had a knack for expressing himself in a way that was both simple and deep. One of his favorite sayings was "Say Less." As he grew older, he used this phrase on many occasions. I began to understand the deeper meaning behind those two simple words. For him, "Say Less" was about finding peace in simplicity.

In the aftermath of his death, his words have taken on a whole new meaning for me. "Say Less" has turned out to be a good reminder to me, meaning that sometimes, things are easier than we make them out to be.

Maybe it means to just take things one day at a time. To appreciate the little things that still make me happy, like a pretty sunset or a walk in the park. Maybe it's about letting go of the "what ifs" and "should haves" and instead focusing on the good memories I have of my son.

Or maybe, just maybe, something else? In my brain, I feel like it's a message from him. A way for him to say, "I'm okay, Mom. We are at peace now. You and everyone else will be okay, too."

Grief, in its raw form, can feel like a bottomless pit. It's easy to get swallowed by the darkness, to feel like there's no room for anything else. But then, there is gratitude.... being grateful for all the blessings in my life and having to spend all those lovely years with my children. It might sound confusing, but the truth is that gratitude can coexist with pain. They may seem like opposing forces, but somehow, they manage to find a fragile balance within the human heart.

Here's how I see it: My gratitude isn't for the tragedy itself, of course. It's for the time I had with my children, for the love we had for each other, and for the memories that continue to bring a smile to my face even through tears. I'm grateful for their laughter, their hugs, and their unique personalities that filled my life with light. I am thankful for the blessings in my life.

I am implying here that the pain doesn't disappear, not entirely. It's always there because it's a deep hurt that never quite goes away. But over time, the pain doesn't remain as bad. It's not so sharp and intense anymore. You must have seen a fire that burns out of control, and then slowly, it dies out with the passage of days and weeks. The flames may still spark occasionally, but they're no longer a raging inferno that threatens to consume everything in its path.

The pain becomes less raw and less draining. The same was the case with me. I could get things done again and go through the motions of life. Sometimes, even happy things happen, like something funny making me laugh even though I'm sad.

It's a slow process, this healing journey. There are good days and bad days. But with each passing day, it gets a little bit easier. It doesn't define me anymore. I am still a mother, even if my children are no longer present. And somehow, I find the strength to keep going, to carry their memory in my heart and continue living for them, even as I mourn their absence.

***

You're probably picking up this book with a heavy heart. Maybe your feelings are all mixed up, like sadness, anger, and confusion all mashed together in a big ball. I understand that grief can be a fierce beast that tears through our sense of security and leaves us feeling utterly lost. I know because I have been there.

Losing someone you love is one of the hardest things a person can go through. It's completely understandable to feel stunned and to experience a lack of control over your emotions, especially given the tragic circumstances. The passing of a loved one leaves a void in a person's life that takes a long time to fill, and the challenges faced in the following days can only compound the pain.

You might feel like everything is upside down, and you can't catch your breath. It's okay to feel overwhelmed and out of control. At first, you might be numb from the shock. Then, all the sadness, anger, and confusion hit you at once. All these feelings are okay. This is a terrible time in your life, and it's okay to grieve in whatever way feels right for you. There's no right or wrong way to heal or grieve. Cry as much as you need to. Yell if it helps. This pain is real, and it's okay to feel it since it deserves to be acknowledged.

But please know this: you are not the only one going through something like this. Many other people have lost someone they love and felt this way. You may feel like your situation is unique, but there are lots of people out there who understand. This book is my story, but it's also a way to let you know you're not alone and how you can understand, deal with, and come out of grief. I'm not trying to make things harder for you by sharing my sadness. Instead, I want to offer you some hope. Even though things feel difficult now, you can get through this.

Transformation and healing are journeys we all take at some point in life. But even when things feel really bad, there's still hope. If you believe things can get better, they will. It won't happen overnight, but with time and care, you'll find yourself laughing again, feeling excited about the future, and carrying the memory of your loved one with love in your heart.

I pray that my heart and the hearts of all the people going through grief and pain become filled with gratitude and healing. I pray that our hearts be filled with goodness, love, and mercy. I pray for peace and wisdom, to get through the darkest nights, and to meet with joy in the morning. I pray for you, the reader, that you always find peace and security. May your journey through grief, however long it takes, lead you to a place of peace and feeling safe. May you find the strength to get through the hard times and discover the happiness that is still in the world. Ameen.

Chapter 3: The Paradox of Grief

"In every heart, there is an inner room where we can hold our greatest treasures and our deepest pain."

— Marianne Williamson

Our life is like a picture with different colors. There are bright colors that show happiness, love, and friendship. But there are also dark colors in this picture, and these colors show loss. Loss can happen in many ways, and it's never something we want. It can feel like an empty seat at a table or like someone you love is no longer there. It can also feel like you can't achieve a dream you had.

Grief is what we naturally feel when loss comes. It's a mix of many emotions all at once. You might feel sad, angry, confused, or like you really miss someone. Your body might also feel the grief, like a pain in your chest or tears that won't stop. Grief doesn't mean you're weak; it means you loved someone or something a lot. Let's have a deeper look into this complex emotion.

The Complex Nature of Grief

Grief is defined by a paradox. On one side, it encompasses a complex and painful whirlwind of thoughts and emotions brought on by the loss of someone dear. On the other side, it is a natural and positive healing process crucial for helping us navigate and release the often unavoidable trauma of loss.

In the simplest terms, grief is an intense emotional reaction to a loss, most commonly felt in the context of death, whether it's the death of a loved one or the individual themselves facing death. Nevertheless, loss can take many forms, and grief can also follow the end of a relationship, the loss of a job, faith, significant material possessions, and more.

The word 'grief' fittingly stems from the Latin 'gravis,' meaning a heavy burden,' as grief arises from the heavy burden of emotions triggered by loss.

Before proceeding, it's essential to understand that grief is not a clinical condition. Assuming you have a clinical issue can be dangerous, as it might alienate you when you already feel isolated, causing you to withdraw or feel ashamed of sharing experiences that are entirely normal.

Everyone goes through grief at some point in their life. It looks different for each person. Your experience is influenced by your own expectations and beliefs about grief, shaped by your unique personality, faith, culture, and life history.

There's no one-size-fits-all path to grief. Cultures express it differently. Some people show their feelings a lot, and others keep them more private.

Sadness in the Grieving Process

Grief is the result of losing something we care about, and sadness is one of its main symptoms. You may argue that love and sadness are inexorably intertwined in this way.

Yes, it's normal to feel depressed during a grieving process. In fact, I would contend that experiencing sadness is essential. However, why is it required? Why is it necessary for the feeling known as sadness to exist at all? Couldn't we just skip over the agony in between and go straight from shock to acceptance of loss?

The response is that sadness is a part of the grieving process. Physically, mentally, emotionally, and socially, it compels us to regroup. We naturally retreat inside when we're depressed. We pull back. We go more slowly. As though our mind says, "Whoa, whoa, whoaaa," and pushes the pause button. "Take a break. I must accept what has transpired."

In actuality, what makes us human is our capacity to

contemplate our own existence. We have a sense of self, unlike other animals. And to feel sorrow, happiness, and love is to be self-aware.

I refer to the required melancholy of sorrow as "sitting in your wound" at times. You give in to your anguish when you sit in its wound. You give in to the need to become more introspective and slow down. You give yourself permission to properly wallow in your suffering. You draw a temporary curtain on the outside, allowing yourself time to process before stepping back in.

The fact that sadness makes other people aware of our innermost thoughts and feelings is another evolutionary explanation for sadness that is still relevant today. Everyone is aware of what a depressed person looks like. He is hunched over. He walks slowly. Both his mouth and eyes droop. It's helpful to be able to read other people's sorrows since it allows us to offer them our support. People used to purposefully draw attention to their grief in order to get sympathy from others centuries ago. They used to get black armbands and went all black for a year. Their hearts were literally on their sleeve.

The Five Stages of Grief

In 1969, psychiatrist Dr. Elisabeth Kübler-Ross proposed five stages of grief in her book 'On Death and

Dying.' According to the American Psychological Association's Dictionary of Psychology, Francis explains that these stages are:

Denial: During this phase, individuals pretend that the loss never happened. When the loss is so severe that the brain is practically overloaded to even start the grieving process, the mind resorts to this natural protection mechanism.

Anger: During this phase, people wonder why anything happened and become visibly angry. When a person experiences an unforeseen or unexpected loss, this period may be especially challenging for them. In order to prevent emotions of powerlessness, anger takes the form of a control-seeking activity that enables people to temporarily take control of their surroundings by acting aggressively.

Bargaining: When everything else seems lost, bargaining becomes a means of finding hope. The thought that our bad actions have somehow, directly or indirectly, contributed to a negative outcome drives us through the bargaining stage of mourning. When faced with helplessness or hopelessness, we often look for understanding and control.

Depression: Anger gives rise to depression as an emotion. Anger and aggressiveness are usually the result of depression in grieving. After a loss, experiencing depression allows people to experience more complex emotions.

Acceptance: The last stage of mourning is acceptance, which comes after we've gone through the preceding phases, given ourselves permission to feel the weight of the loss, and discovered a means to go on by adopting more constructive coping mechanisms and accepting the things that we can control. Acceptance does not imply forgetting or complete recovery from a loss. Even after acknowledging the pain, we could still regress into earlier phases.

It's important to remember that sorrow isn't always as linear or well-structured as this theory implies. Because every person responds to loss differently, and every person's experience of grieving is unique.

Is Guilt a Part of My Grieving Process Too?

You know that feeling you get when you beat yourself up for not being perfect? That ache in your gut that whispers, "I should've done more"? That's guilt, and it can show up big time when you're grieving something important.

Grief and guilt can be like roommates who share a way too small apartment - they just seem to bump into each other all the time. You're already dealing with a huge loss, and then guilt piles on, making you feel even worse. It might sound like this: "Why didn't I say goodbye better?" or "Maybe if I had done things differently..."

The thing is, grief is messy, and it's normal to feel like you didn't do enough, even if that's not quite true. You might blame yourself for things that were out of your control or avoid places that remind you of what's gone. That's okay. It doesn't mean you're weak or crazy.

Some folks might tell you guilt isn't a 'real' part of grief because it's not on Kübler-Ross proposed five stages of grief. But that is just a guide, not a rulebook. Everyone grieves differently, and there's no right or wrong way to feel. When something big happens, our brains go into overdrive, trying to understand it. Sometimes, that means revisiting the past and finding things that make us feel guilty. It's part of the process.

It's normal to feel both grief and guilt after a loss, and it can happen for all sorts of reasons. Maybe your family always taught you to take care of your elders, and now you wonder if you did enough. Or maybe you keep replaying moments in your head, wishing you could go back and do something differently.

Guilt can hold you back from healing. Some people who feel guilty after a loss can likely get stuck in a place where the grief just won't ease up, even after a year. That kind of grief can even lead to depression. So, while guilt is totally normal, it's important not to let it take the wheel.

Why Is Grief So Confusing Sometimes?

Loss can feel like a sucker punch, not just to your emotions but to your whole way of thinking. It's no surprise, then, that your mind might feel foggy, forgetful, and even confused. Your brain might be struggling to keep up with everything that's happened. And let's be honest, that can be scary and unnerving.

Hearts that are grieving typically feel a little confused. Here are five essential items to keep in mind if you're feeling lost.

- *Confusion over grief is typical.* When we experience loss, our hearts break, and we feel everything. Some people are able to control some of their emotions, but they still occasionally find unhealthy ways for them to come out. Some people openly express their feelings but in a way that isn't beneficial to them.

- Others pick up coping mechanisms for grieving that reflect their identities and their bonds with the deceased. Confusion is a natural reaction to this wild mix of sadness, rage, worry, dread, guilt, and fury.

- *You have no prior experience here.* This is unfamiliar ground. The landscape you find yourself in, regardless of your fixed notions about it, is not what you anticipated or envisaged. You could never have been entirely prepared for this. It makes sense why you get puzzled sometimes.

- *Your Brain is Doing Its Best.* Even though things seem foggy, your brain is working hard. It's trying to understand this new situation, this world without your loved one. It's processing the pain in your heart and the changes in your daily life. Give yourself some credit – your brain is a pretty amazing thing, even when it feels scrambled.

- *Be Patient With Yourself.* Grief isn't a race. It's a marathon with ups and downs, twists and turns. Be patient with yourself as you go through this journey. There will be good days and bad days, confusing moments and moments of clarity. It's all part of the process.

- *You're Not Alone.* Remember, you're not some emotionless robot. You're a grieving human being who's allowed to feel everything – even the confusion. Take a deep breath and give yourself permission not to have all the answers. Loss is confusing, but you're strong. This is a difficult time, and it's okay to be confused. But remember, you're stronger than you think. You've got this.

Why Does Grief Make Me Feel Lonely and Hopeless?

When my children passed away, I felt lonely. I thought I was the only person in the world who was going through this, and often, I would be around people all day and still feel lonely.

But now that I look back and think about it, it is rather common to experience loneliness during a period of bereavement. We can be taken aback by the weight of sadness at first because it can cause both emotional and bodily reactions in us. Not only can the physical absence of someone make you feel alone, but it may also rob you of their emotional and social support.

Everyone expects things to get better with time, so when they don't, you may feel as though something is wrong with you. This can make you feel hopeless, as can those around you. It's critical to keep in mind that grieving is a continuous process. You will occasionally have more intense, sorrowful reactions. That does not imply that your grieving process is beginning anew; rather, it is a valley you are passing through.

It's likely that you will always feel a part of the loss.

However, there are strategies to help you deal with the loneliness as you proceed through your grieving process and learn to live with the loss. It will take some time, so please be patient with yourself while you adjust to your new normal.

Grief Can Feel Like Freefalling

Have you ever done one of those internet searches for 'fear symptoms'? Turns out, a lot of them line up perfectly with grief. It makes sense, really. Grief throws you into this crazy world of uncertainty as if the ground ripped out from under your feet.

We all have these ideas about what makes life predictable, right? Be good, take care of yourself, love others, and everything will (hopefully) work out. But then loss hits, and suddenly, all those assumptions get tossed out the window.

You might feel lost and stumbling, questioning yourself like, *Who am I even anymore? What do I do next? How do I pick up the pieces and move forward if that's even what I want?* It's like everything you thought you knew about life just exploded. Nothing feels safe; nothing feels certain. You're questioning everything, everyone, even yourself.

Grief can be so intense it starts to feel real. Like the fear itself becomes your world, this suffocating bubble that you can't escape. It's your worst fear come true, and you're stuck in the middle of it, not sure which way is up.

Fear and grief can feel like tangled wires in your brain, both sending out those same warning signals – racing heart, sweaty palms, the whole shebang. But there's a key difference: fear is all about a threat you can kind of make out, even if it's a bit scary and nonsensical. Grief, on the other hand, is stuck on replay, dwelling on a loss that already happened.

Fear makes you wanna slam on the brakes, scared to make a move because you're not sure you can trust yourself to make the right call. It keeps you stuck, afraid to get hurt again. Fear gets a bad rap, but it's actually trying to help, even if it's annoying. The key is not to let it become your boss. Real courage isn't the absence of fear; it's staring that fear right in the face and saying, "Bring it on!" It's about picking yourself up after a loss and saying "yes" to life again, even when your heart feels like it's gonna shatter.

Nudge yourself whenever you get stuck in fear mode, paralyzed by indecision. Say to yourself, "Just go for it! What's the worst that could happen?"

Regret While Grieving

One of the most common words I heard myself saying or thinking during my grieving journey is 'regret.' Regret stings. It's a deep emotional and mental ache. The problem is it can get stuck on repeat, holding you hostage in the past.

Regret can be about things you did or things you didn't do. It's that awful feeling of being stuck between a rock and a hard place, damned if you did, damned if you didn't. When you're grieving a loved one, regret can latch onto those past experiences you shared. It's the constant wishing, the "what ifs" swirling in your head. Maybe a decision you made led to something painful, or you said something you wish you could take back.

We all want to understand our grief and make sense of this unbearable pain. Maybe if we could just figure it out, it wouldn't hurt so much. But sometimes, those regretful thoughts creep in because your heart aches for that connection you've lost.

It might sound crazy, but for some people, regret is actually a necessary part of working through grief. It's like your mind's way of processing everything, even if it feels like self-punishment.

I wish I could somehow erase your regret. But trust me, there might be something important to learn from it. Instead of pushing it away, try listening to what it's trying to tell you. Maybe it's about forgiveness, acceptance, or simply cherishing the memories you have.

We all do it: take that one thing we regret and turn it into a giant label that defines us. But the thing is that clinging to regret only makes grief worse. So, how do we break free?

Reframe the Story

Let's say you regret something you did (or didn't do) related to your loved one. Tell yourself that you made the best choice you could at the time. You had all that information, all those circumstances swirling around. It's time to cut yourself some slack and believe you did the best you could with what you had.

This 'reframing' takes practice. It might feel fake at first, like you're telling yourself a lie. But keep at it, write it down, stick it somewhere you'll see it all day. The more you repeat it, the more it'll sink in. Eventually, the regret won't sting as much, and you'll believe you did the best you could.

Forgive Yourself (It's Okay If It Takes Time)

Forgiveness is a journey, not a destination. It's hard, and it takes patience. But chances are, you're already on this path, even if you don't realize it.

It's about shifting your perspective and being kind and gentle with yourself. It's about finding your way back to self-love, which is hard after any loss. There's a whole science to forgiveness, but for now, remember this: forgiveness is a choice, not a feeling. Saying "I can't forgive myself" is really saying "I won't." It's a tough pill to swallow, but it's true.

The good news is that self-compassion can pave the way for forgiveness. Remind yourself of all the love and care you gave your loved one. Write it down if it helps. Accepting what happened is also key. Acceptance is a decision you make, and it can help you forgive yourself.

The hope is that you look at the facts, accept that you did something wrong, apologize, choose to forgive yourself and do better in the future. Let yourself off the hook. You deserve it.

Why Do You Feel Numb?

When someone passes away, some of us get sad. Anger is a feeling shared by some of us. However, others of us experience nothing at all. 'Inhibited grieving,' a form of grief marked by repressed feelings, has been associated with emotional numbness. This kind of grieving might not be appropriate for how society wants us to act following a loss.

Although it can be challenging to identify emotional numbness when it occurs, people frequently express uncertainty when reflecting on the initial phases of their mourning. *How come I didn't cry? It feels impossible now to control my emotions; how could I have done it then?*

I like to consider it as a covert means of self-defense. In the short run, emotional numbness can be beneficial in certain ways. There are things to get organized, family and friends to get in touch with, and a funeral to plan. I guess we can get through it all by temporarily blocking off our emotions and concentrating on things that are useful.

In reality, don't immediately reach out to individuals following a death because of that emotional numbness. According to an article published by a Bereavement Coordinator, this is not necessarily the most effective period for treatment; wait eight weeks to allow them to start processing what has happened.[1] Emotionally numb people frequently worry about what other people may think.

Maybe you didn't cry at the funeral, and that's okay. It doesn't mean you didn't care, and it doesn't change the bond you shared with the person you lost. Sometimes, people might comment on how "strong" you seem. Trust me, they don't mean to downplay your grief. They probably just want to offer support in the only way they know how. You might see others crying openly, expressing their emotions freely. That's okay,

---

[1] Marie Curie. (2002). *Emotional numbness and grief.* Retrieved August 9, 2024, from https://www.mariecurie.org.uk/talkabout/articles/emotional-numbness-grief/346166

too. Everyone grieves differently. Just because you're numb right now doesn't mean you won't feel the weight of this loss later. Over time, grief changes, and the emotional numbness usually goes away. Since each person is unique, it's difficult to predict when numbness will go away.

Grief has its ups and downs, and loneliness can get worse before getting better while a person is grieving. This is accurate for the majority of people, according to research by University of Memphis psychology professor Robert Neimeyer.[2] It's usual to endure heightened grieving for six to eight months following the death before seeing a decrease in those sentiments. It's also possible for your grief to resurface at the 12- and 24-month marks.

Riding the Waves of Grief

Grief, like the ocean, can be a powerful force. It crashes in waves of devastating emotions, pulling us undercurrents of misery and leaving us gasping for air on the shore of loss. But just as the ocean holds the potential for calm coves and gentle currents, so too does grief offer moments of

---

[2] Neimeyer, R. (2005). Grief, loss, and the quest for meaning: Narrative contributions to bereavement care. *Bereavement Care, 24*(2), 27-30.

peace and the strength to go through its depths.

The key lies in allowing ourselves to feel the waves — the sorrow, the anger, the fear. Ignoring these emotions only strengthens their hold. By acknowledging them, we begin to understand them and find ways to move through them.

Yet, we don't have to weather this storm alone. This journey requires a sturdy vessel – a strong support system and, of course, self-care. Nourishing our bodies with healthy food and rest and nurturing our minds with activities we enjoy are essential for staying afloat. We'll look into this self-care aspect later in the book. For now, all I have to say is the storm inside won't subside if you ignore it. Realize it, accept it, and let it go with time.

Chapter 4: Don't Bottle it Up

"You know what truly aches? Having so much inside you and not having the slightest clue of how to pour it out."

— Karen Quan

They say grief is a journey. They say it's a path with twists and turns, uphill climbs, and unexpected meadows. One of the most important things I've learned on this journey is this: don't be afraid to feel. All the emotions, the good, the bad, and the downright ugly – they all deserve a place at the table.

Pushing down your emotions might seem like the easier option at first. A shield against the pain inside your heart. But trust me, those emotions have a way of bubbling up eventually, often at the most inconvenient times. It's better to acknowledge them, to let them wash over you, however messy it may feel.

Sometimes, the grief feels like a tidal wave, knocking me off my feet and dragging me under. It leaves me gasping for air. Other times, it feels like a low hum.

There are days when there's guilt. The inexorable "what ifs" and "should haves" that gnaw at the soul. The truth is, we can't change the past. Dwelling on it only prolongs the pain. Instead, try to focus on the love you shared and the happy memories.

Grief can also manifest in unexpected ways. For some, it can come in the form of a complete lack of appetite. Other people might experience sleep disturbances, fatigue, or even physical pain. It's important to listen to your body and take care of yourself during this time.

Don't be afraid to ask for help. Whether it's a therapist, a grief support group, or just a friend to listen to, having a support system can make a world of difference. Talking it out can help you process your emotions and feel less alone.

As I stated earlier, there's no right or wrong way to grieve. Allow yourself to feel the full spectrum of emotions, even the ones that feel uncomfortable. Cry if you need to, scream if it helps. This journey is yours, and there's no set timeline for healing. Let yourself grieve at your own pace, and don't be afraid to seek support along the way. Remember, the colors of grief may be dark now, but with time, they will begin to lighten, and brighter hues will peek through.

Emotional Processing

We've talked about acknowledging and experiencing the full spectrum of emotions in grief. But there's another crucial step – processing those emotions. Processing is like an engine that propels you forward on your healing journey. Ignoring your emotions might seem easier at first, like putting a lid on a boiling pot. But the pressure will build, and eventually, it will explode in an unhealthy way.

Processing your emotions allows you to understand them, work through them, and eventually, let them go, just like taking the lid off the pot and letting the steam out in a controlled manner. It might still be hot and uncomfortable, but it's a much safer way to release the pressure.

In a more literal scenario, emotional processing is "a process that ... constitutes the essence of recovery or emotional processing."

Most people handle life's distressing events without lasting issues. As Jack Rachman, the psychologist who defined emotional processing in 1980, noted, this successful processing is the typical experience. But what if the event is incredibly overwhelming, or the person simply can't cope? Then what?

The event might be something recent, like a car accident, a divorce, or a family member's death, that the person is struggling to handle. Or it could be something that happened a long time ago, which was never properly addressed at the time and was pushed away, hoping it would vanish forever, but its impact continues. This past event could have been bullying at school, sexual abuse, parents' separation, or other troubling experiences.

For some people, therapy can be an effective means of managing difficult emotions. This is where Emotional Processing Therapy plays a role. The aim of Emotional Processing Therapy is to assist people in fully dealing with recent or past upsetting events, helping them achieve a sense of calm where they no longer feel emotionally distressed.

Learning to recognize and control our emotions in a healthy way is the foundation of emotion processing, and it entails the following:

Pausing

When anything happens, stand back and give yourself some time to absorb the situation before responding. Depending on the circumstances and the strength of the emotion you are experiencing, this could be simple or difficult to accomplish.

It could be tough not to beep your horn and give the person a nasty look, for instance, if they cut you off in traffic. But if you stop and consider what transpired, you may find that the other car was rushing and didn't realize they had cut you off.

This knowledge can assist you in controlling your rage

and avoiding overreacting. Taking a few deep breaths, counting to ten (or twenty, or hundred!), removing yourself from the situation if at all feasible, and visualizing a peaceful image or scenario are some useful techniques to stop and process your feelings.

Acknowledging

It's a piece of typical advice from people to "just let it out" when you're upset. Pent-up emotions, however, might occasionally seem as though they're taking on a life of their own. It could be helpful to identify and label your emotions if you're having trouble controlling them. You'll regain some control and be able to identify potential triggers for your reactions if you do this. To alleviate feelings of overwhelm, you could tell yourself something like, "I'm feeling overwhelmed by this situation."

Accept your feelings without passing judgment. Recognize that you are experiencing feelings such as anger, sadness, anxiety, etc., and don't give them any significance. Rather than being enmeshed in your emotions, it can be helpful to examine them with curiosity and as an outsider.

After recognizing the emotion, you can begin to investigate the cause of your feelings and potential solutions. Meanwhile, keep in mind that experiencing emotions is normal and contributes to our humanity.

We already discussed the fact that emotions are neither 'good' nor 'bad.' It's how you react to them, is good or bad. Knowing this makes it possible for you to be more accepting of all of your feelings, even the ones you may consider to be unpleasant.

Labeling

Try to name the feelings you're experiencing as you're paying attention to what's going on inside of you. In and of itself, this can be beneficial since it helps you make sense of what happened to you.

Speaking aloud about your feelings to someone or to yourself can also be helpful. This small action can help reduce the intensity of unpleasant feelings.

Expressing

You may discover that you need to vent your feelings in a healthy way after giving them some time to settle. Although everyone's interpretation of this will change, some typical instances include neglecting your basic needs, which can often contribute to emotional instability. To maintain emotional well-being, prioritize self-care by ensuring consistent, balanced nutrition, enough rest, regular exercise, and spending time outdoors. These fundamental actions can suggestively reduce your vulnerability to emotional outbursts.

The Benefits of Processing Emotions

The ability to manage emotions in a healthy way has several advantages. Some of the benefits are:

Greater Emotional Intelligence

The capacity to recognize, comprehend, and manage your own emotions, as well as those of others, is known as emotional intelligence. People having high emotional intelligence are more adept at handling difficult circumstances in their personal and occupational spheres.

Increased Self-Awareness

When we take the time to understand our emotions, we can identify their triggers and the situations that cause them. This self-awareness allows us to recognize patterns and predict how we might react in the future.

For instance, if you have a history of physical abuse, loud noises might trigger intense fear and flashbacks. By recognizing this pattern, you can develop strategies to manage your environment and seek professional help to address the underlying trauma.

Building Resilience

Processing emotions helps us develop resilience, which is the ability to bounce back from challenges. By understanding our emotions, we can develop healthy coping mechanisms to deal with difficult situations.

For example, if you acknowledge feeling overwhelmed after a fight with a friend, you can use coping mechanisms like taking a walk or journaling to process those emotions and move forward in a healthier way.

Sharpening Coping Skills

As we process emotions, we gain experience in managing them. This experience helps us develop a toolbox of coping skills that we can use in different situations.

These skills can include things like relaxation techniques, healthy communication strategies, or seeking support from others. The more we process our emotions, the more comfortable we become using these skills effectively.

Gratitude

Those who have good emotional regulation skills typically have higher levels of gratitude in life. This is most likely due to the fact that they are better able to appreciate the good times and are less prone to become mired in unpleasant feelings.

Improved Relationships

People who can manage their emotions well typically lead happier and healthier relationships. This is probably due to the fact that they can express their wants and resolve conflicts more effectively.

Improved Sleep

The quality of your sleep can be greatly impacted by the things that keep you up at night, such as worry and anxiety. People who are able to manage their emotions well typically get better sleep because they are less likely to be disturbed by unfavorable thoughts and emotions.

What Are Some Unhealthy Ways to Cope With Emotions?

It's okay to have difficult emotions, but some people deal with them in destructive ways. Some common unhealthy coping mechanisms include:

Bottling Up Emotions

Suppressing emotions instead of addressing them can lead to emotional outbursts, physical health problems, and difficulty concentrating. When you push down your feelings, they don't disappear. They can build up over time and, sooner or later, might erupt in unhealthy ways, such as anger outbursts or anxiety attacks.

Isolation

When you're hurting, it can be easy to withdraw and hide from the world. But shutting people out can make you feel even lonelier and more overwhelmed. Remember, you don't have to face things alone.

Substance Abuse

Turning to alcohol, drugs, or food might seem like a quick and easy way to escape your feelings. It might even work in the short term. But substances don't actually deal with your problems and should never be the solution. In fact, they can make things worse in the long run. Substance abuse can lead to addiction, health problems, and damaged relationships. It can also make it harder to cope with your emotions in a healthy way - the very thing you were trying to avoid in the first place.

Taking it Out on Others

Venting to a trusted friend can be healthy, but there's a difference between venting and lashing out. When you're feeling angry or frustrated, it's tempting to blame the people closest to you. You might snap at your partner for something small or give your friend a cold shoulder because of something they said. But blaming others for your feelings won't make you feel better in the long run. It will only damage your relationships and make the people you care about walk on eggshells around you.

What is Emotional Release?

Emotional release is about freeing yourself from the grip of negative feelings, like letting out a big sigh of relief after holding your breath for too long. Sometimes, this happens naturally, like when you burst into tears after a stressful day or event. While it might feel overwhelming in the moment, it often leads to a sense of calm and clarity afterward.

Many people actively seek ways to release their emotions in healthy ways. Therapy can provide a safe space to explore and process difficult emotions. There are also specific techniques like journaling that can help you connect with your emotions and let them go.

If you're feeling stuck in a cycle of anger, fear, or sadness, emotional release can be a game-changer. It's a way to break free from the emotional baggage that's been weighing you down. By understanding and experiencing emotional release, you can gain a deeper sense of control over your emotions. This can lead to a more peaceful and fulfilling life, with greater resilience in the face of challenges.

The Importance of Emotional Validation

Have you ever questioned your own feelings, wondering if your reactions were too strong or misguided? Your emotions are valid and important components of your personal journey. In a world that often pressures us to suppress our feelings, embracing them is key to understanding ourselves and growing.

Science supports the idea that acknowledging your emotions is helpful for mental health. When you validate your feelings, you're telling yourself that what you're experiencing is real and important. This self-acceptance is vital for healing and developing healthier emotional responses.

Recognizing your emotions also deepens connections with others. When we recognize and express our feelings openly and honestly, we create space for empathy and compassion. Our loved ones can connect with us on a deeper level. We, in turn, can learn to validate the emotions of others, creating a safe space for open communication and mutual understanding. This builds a world where vulnerability isn't a weakness but a strength that strengthens our connections with others.

Remember, validating your emotions doesn't mean

justifying any action. It's about using your feelings as a starting point for thoughtful decision-making.

The Shattered World of Grief and Integration of Loss

Life seems to divide into two phases: before and after when someone passes away or you suffer another terrible loss. Experiencing grief in the initial days and weeks after a loss is all-consuming. You have an almost compulsive desire to revisit the past and the idealized version of life that once existed. You're overcome with utter astonishment, uncertainty, and anxiety about your ability to survive in this broken, 'after-loss' world of yours. The future frequently appears to be an empty abyss, and the pain seems to never stop.

In the beginning, memories of the person may only cause pain. And yet, since it seems like all you have left, people frequently feel compelled to cling to the reminders. Even if those things can occasionally act as overpowering memories of their absence, you want to save everything they touched, their scent, and the sound of their voice. You may replay those experiences over and over in your head, attempting to make the memories stick. To avoid looking around at the present and future when your loved one is missing, you might spend a lot of time in the past.

The emotions of grieving can be terrifying. It's normal to fear that the flood of grief-related feelings will overwhelm you. People fight back against grief in an attempt to manage the severity of these feelings. You may discover that you steer clear of anything that triggers the discomfort. You can be doing the exact opposite of clinging to every indication of your loved one. You might be trying not to think about the loss, avoiding places and things that could make you cry, or ignoring those reminders in an effort to control your emotions.

And it may appear differently every day or every week, leaving you to wonder, *When will this end? When will I be able to 'move on' and find acceptance at last?*

Even though it's difficult to accept, we manage to get through the initial days following a loss, one day at a time. One breath at a time, sometimes. Though the agony never goes away, our brains gradually begin to process the reality of our loved one's absence. One of the theories of grief, the Dual Process Model of bereavement, examines how we manage both restoration-oriented stressors (the realistic daily tasks of reconstructing life after loss) and loss-oriented stressors (our memories and connections to our loved ones and the pain of our loss). We oscillate between immersing ourselves in our grief and tending to the practicalities of daily life. There's no linear path, no clear endpoint. Acceptance doesn't mean forgetting but rather integrating the loss into the fabric of our new reality.

We begin to figure out how to live a meaningful and balanced life without our loved ones as we gradually get back into routines. Many people eventually come to realize that they wish to return to a place of prosperity and that they want to carry their loved one's memory with them. Early grief coping mechanisms frequently work against such objectives. It is impossible to have a meaningful present if one is frantically clinging to every reminder and living in the past and the agony. However, attempting bravely to block out painful memories or numb unpleasant emotions, as well as disregarding the past, prevents us from experiencing an emotional attachment to our loved one's memory in the present time. They carve up the world such that we are either overcome with sadness or choose to ignore it and the memories of our loved ones. Both are unsustainable.

So, what does it really mean by 'integrating grief?'

Most people who experience sadness eventually come to terms with how it has altered them. Nothing will return to 'normal.' We have to allow the loss to stay in order to manage the complex feelings of bereavement, maintain a connection to our loved one's memories, and lead meaningful lives. That is what I call 'integrating grief.'

Integrated grief is a type of grieving that coexists with your life and continues to be a part of it without taking over or controlling it. I understand that it could feel incomprehensible right now. However, as you learn to manage the complicated feelings of loss and transform your perspective on it, the gap between 'functioning' and grieving will gradually narrow. Your identity is impacted by grief, which modifies your priorities, duties, and connections. Letting go of the person you were before the loss and accepting the person you are now - a person altered by grief, frequently in both positive and negative ways - is the key to integrating grief. It gets easier to move on to a new life as you grow to understand what it means to live with the memories of someone who has passed away.

Understanding Complicated Grief

Continued sadness following a loss is referred to as complicated grief. It can interfere with your everyday life by causing strong feelings and obsessive thoughts that don't go away. You might feel overwhelmed by the loss, constantly preoccupied with it, feeling as though you had to push away or avoid memories of a loss and struggle to move forward.

Treatment for complicated grief often involves cognitive behavioral therapy (CBT) to help you process your emotions, adjust to life without your loved one, and gradually return to your normal activities. Support groups can also provide comfort and understanding. In some cases, medication may be prescribed to manage symptoms, but please don't take anything on your own to cater to or suppress your feelings.

While healing takes time, it's essential to remember that everyone's journey is unique. With the right support, you can work through complicated grief and find a way to live with your loss.

You might now question if complicated grief can be prevented or avoided. Well, there's no guaranteed way to shield yourself entirely from the complexities of grief. However, building a support network of loved ones and speaking with a mental health professional following a loss can help lower your risk of experiencing complicated grief.

The Power of Connection and Support

Even though grieving can feel daunting and isolating at first, in the days that follow, having supportive, meaningful connections becomes important. You can discuss your feelings in a consoling and understanding environment when you have connections. Grieving with someone who gets it - a friend, family member, or support group, for example - makes your suffering feel real, helps you accept it, and makes you feel less alone. Through these relationships, you can take comfort in the knowledge that others who are traveling similar pathways also experience the same emotions as you, which might ultimately make you feel normal.

Connections give us strength and resilience. Grieving is tough, but having supportive people around can help you cope. These bonds can offer practical help, like assisting with daily tasks or just being there for you. Sharing the burden can make grief easier to handle and prevent overwhelming despair.

Connections also help us remember the person who has died. Sharing memories and stories keeps the memories alive, ensuring they remain in the hearts and minds of those left behind.

Personal Growth Through Grief

The entire notion that we may learn from our experiences while we are grieving might feel so offensive. Who would want to grow at such a high cost, after all? It nearly appears as though someone is abrasively advising us to find the bright side.

We can, however, actually grow. Regarding loss, we are powerless. Regarding the ensuing grief, we are powerless. Within our loss, we do have one option, though. Grief will transform us. Never again will things be the same. Never again will we be the same. It is not a question of if we will change but rather how we will change. Either we can grow up, or we can grow down.

In their writings, psychologists Richard Tedeschi and Larry Calhoun discuss a concept they refer to as "post-traumatic growth." They understand that experiencing loss challenges our preconceptions of reality. We must reevaluate both our worldview and our way of living in the new world if we are to rebuild our own and survive. Growth results from such reevaluation.

There are several ways to experience this growth. We can come out of it with a deeper understanding of life. We can value our connections more now that we are aware of how short life can be. We might rearrange our priorities. We understand that no one who passed away ever regretted not working longer or using the internet more.

We start by admitting that in order to move past this loss and go forward, we must adapt and evolve. Sometimes, it is helpful to look back on these developments and acknowledge, if not truly appreciate, the personal growth we have undergone.

Maybe we should empower ourselves. Here, our own language can be helpful. We can consider that even in the midst of grieving, we have options. Instead of viewing our difficulties as puzzles that baffle us, we might view them as obstacles we must overcome.

We may build upon our strengths. Think back to your past tragedies and crises in life. What made those crises easier for you to overcome? You might now use whatever has previously aided you. But occasionally, you need to redefine those strengths.

Although growth may not be a good substitute for loss, it surely has some hope to get better.

We've explored what entails bottling up our emotions. But perhaps the most surprising truth is that allowing ourselves to feel, truly feel, is one of the first steps to live a normal life again. By accepting our emotions, we open ourselves to growth, connection, and a deeper understanding of ourselves and the world around us. So, the next time a wave of emotion washes over you, don't resist it. Let it flow, and see where it takes you.

Chapter 5: The Wolf in A Sheep's Clothing - Anger

The length of time it takes you to mourn a loved one who has passed away depends on how you define grief in your mind. Many come to the belief that grieving is mechanical in some way and needs to be divided into manageable chunks and completed within a set amount of time.

I've grieved the losses of loved ones who passed away suddenly and in a timely manner, and I've come to the conclusion that grief is a phase of love that needs to be embraced until we can accept it and peacefully carry the memories of our time spent together.

We mourn because we are in love.

If there is no love, there will be no grief.

The more we care about someone and the longer we know them, the harder it hurts when they're gone. Parents and kids usually have the closest and longest relationships. Some people even live with their partners longer than anyone else.

We don't always say it, but we know that one of us will

die before the other when we love someone. It's a sad part of loving. When someone we love dies, our love for them changes, but it doesn't disappear. We deal with the pain and sadness until we can accept it. Then, we can hold onto the good memories and what we learned from that love.

Instead of thinking of grief as bad or harmful, we should see it as something that can teach us important things about love.

But it's easier said than done. When the sudden shock and pain of losing that dear human hits us, we all react to it differently. And one of those reactions that can be considered intense and very dangerous is anger.

Anger Might Mask Your Grief

Most people think of sadness when they think of grief, but being angry is also a very common reaction during the grieving process. When you lose someone you love, you might get angry and ask yourself why it happened. You could be mad at yourself, everyone around you, the person who died, or simply how things happened.

We can also feel sad and mad when we lose other important things, like a friend, job, or something associated with our identity. When we're sad, we might want to be quiet and still instead of doing things. We might feel tired and heavy, and it can feel like something is pulling us down and keeping us in one place.

Tension around our eyes from crying, wanting to cry, or just wanting to close them might occur when we are grieving. We may want to sleep yet find it impossible. We may carry fatigue in our bodies and minds. Both could affect our hunger. It could also result in an upset stomach. Grief can make your chest or throat feel tight or empty. We could be taken back to previous losses while we are mourning, feeling the pain and sorrow that comes with them all over again. This can be particularly true if we haven't dealt with our sadness over the loss in an open and sincere manner. We might try to imagine what our life will be like from now on.

When we're grieving, it can feel like the world is moving too fast. We might wonder how everyone else can carry on when we're hurting so much. Even with people around us, we can feel really alone. Because grief is so hard, we might try to hide it or forget about it. Some people get really busy to stop thinking about their loss. Others might try to replace what they lost, like getting a new dog that looks the same as the one that died and naming it the same as well.

On the other hand, unacknowledged grief simply seeks attention and serves to intensify agony on an emotional and physical level. Emotional numbness, mild depression, low energy, and decreased motivation might result from suppressed grief. Furthermore, it could exacerbate cardiac issues and result in worry, despair, or even panic attacks.

Anger may also be a potent diversion from mourning for a lot of people. Anger is a powerful feeling that focuses our attention on something outward or someone that we believe is causing our anger. People also try to shield themselves from the excruciating anguish of sadness by focusing their attention in other directions.

I've seen people get this kind of rage when they lose a loved one, get dumped by a spouse, or suffer from a disease or accident that prevents them from achieving their goals. Some people choose to hold onto their anger rather than face the sorrow that comes with admitting the situation. Certain individuals may harbor animosity towards minor setbacks that occur in their daily lives, such as being cut off by a car ahead of them, the cashier making an error, or the contractor being late by an hour. In each situation, they could find it difficult to let go of the notion that others should behave in a certain way.

You might think letting off steam is good for you or that everyone else is too thin-skinned. Maybe you believe anger is your right or even a power move. But the truth is, anger often backfires. It can damage your image, cloud your thinking, and hold you back. There is no doubt that allowing anger to consume you can be detrimental to your overall well-being.

When Anger Becomes a Prison

Anger can be like a storm inside us. It can make us say things we don't mean, and it can certainly make us do things we regret later. This can lead to arguments with people we care about. When we're angry, we might also want to be alone. This can push people away and make us feel even more upset like we're building a wall around ourselves.

Anger can cloud our judgment and make it difficult to think clearly. As I said, when we're angry, we're more likely to say or do things that we would regret later. This can damage our relationships with others and make it harder to get the support we need. Not everyone understands what we're going through. After all, we're all humans. It's important to remember that anger is a normal emotion, but it's important to find healthy ways to express it.

When someone we love dies, anger can be a strong and confusing feeling. It can feel like a betrayal, a punishment for something we didn't do. We might be angry at the person who died for leaving us. We might be angry at ourselves for not being able to prevent their death. All of these feelings are normal to occur, and they don't make us bad people unless we realize that they are just feelings out of grief.

Anger can create a defensive posture that deters our ability to learn from our experiences. We may become resistant to feedback or support. This isolation can limit our exposure to different viewpoints and deprive us of valuable lessons. It can make it hard to talk to others and ask for help. We might withdraw from our friends and family, or we might lash out at them. We might feel like we're a burden or that no one understands what we're going through.

But it's important to remember that our friends and family, more often than not, want to help. They can offer comfort and support, which can make the pain a little easier to bear. Pushing them away because of anger can make the grieving process harder and longer.

Moreover, it's difficult to make space for other emotions if we're dealing with anger all the time during our grieving process. These other feelings, such as sadness, grief, or longing, are essential parts of the healing process. By focusing solely on anger, we're essentially putting these other emotions on hold. Over time, this can lead to a buildup of suppressed feelings, which can manifest in unhealthy ways.

Think about it. What would happen if you tried to bandage a wound without cleaning it first? It might become worse over time, won't it? Similarly, anger might numb the pain temporarily, but it doesn't address the underlying issue. To heal, we need to allow ourselves to feel the full range of emotions, including the painful ones. Then, we can begin to process our loss and move forward.

Anger as a Block to Growth

Anger can be a formidable obstacle to personal growth, especially in the context of grief. When we're caught in the grip of anger, our focus narrows, and our ability to see the bigger picture diminishes. We become less receptive to new perspectives, ideas, or insights.

There is no doubt that, indeed, grief is a complex journey of learning and transformation. It offers opportunities for personal growth, such as developing resilience, empathy, and a deeper appreciation for the everyday blessings in our lives that often go overlooked. However, anger can overshadow these opportunities. By consuming our thoughts and energy, it prevents us from looking into the deeper meanings of our loss and how it can shape our lives moving forward.

Ultimately, anger can trap us in a cycle of pain and resentment and hinder our ability to move forward and find healing.

The Toll of Anger

When we feel really mad, our bodies go into high gear. Our heart starts pounding, our breathing speeds up, and our muscles tense up. Our blood pressure rises, and our body releases a surge of stress hormones, such as adrenaline and cortisol. These hormones prepare us for action, but they can also have negative effects on our body and mind if we experience them too often or for too long. For example, chronic stress can weaken our immune system, increase our risk of heart disease, and contribute to mental health problems such as anxiety and depression. These changes can feel strong and even scary, and if they happen too much, they can wear down our bodies over time.

The Thin Line Between Coping and Crumbling

There are two primary types of coping mechanisms: adaptive and maladaptive. Healthy coping strategies, i.e., adaptive, help tackle problems while also keeping stress and harm in check. On the other hand, unhealthy coping mechanisms might offer some immediate relief, but they don't address the root of the issues and can lead to more stress and long-term damage.

Avoiding maladaptive coping mechanisms might be challenging because they frequently appear to be beneficial. Even while they might offer some brief relief, this comfort is fleeting and may cause other issues in the future. Though initially benign, these habits have the potential to negatively impact both your physical and mental well-being.

While coping mechanisms in and of themselves aren't always harmful, over-reliance on them can turn them into a crutch and have unfavorable consequences. They may appear advantageous at first, but they have the potential to become harmful over time.

Here are some coping mechanisms that can be unhealthy or maladaptive:

Isolation and Excessive Reliance on Others

Isolating yourself or leaning too heavily on others can both be problematic. When you're feeling overwhelmed or frustrated with people, it might seem like the best option to shut yourself off from the world. However, staying disconnected from others for too long can harm your mental and physical health, as social interaction is important as well.

On the flip side, relying excessively on others can be just as harmful. It's great to have support, but if your self-worth and validation depend too much on family or friends, your self-esteem can become fragile. When your happiness relies entirely on having others around, facing challenges without them becomes much more difficult.

Making Hasty Decisions and/or Catastrophizing

Jumping to conclusions or catastrophizing is one way people try to handle decisions and problems, but it can backfire. If you find yourself constantly assuming the worst-case scenario to avoid any potential hurt, you might be catastrophizing. This kind of thinking can skew your perception, making it hard to see positive aspects and leading to decisions based on fear rather than a balanced view.

Scrolling Down to the Bottom

Although social networking has become a popular way for people to vent their stress, it frequently makes matters worse rather than better. This is what doomscrolling is. It's when you keep scrolling through social media even though it's just adding to your stress with negative news and emotions. Instead of providing relief, it often makes you feel more overwhelmed.

Not Thinking About the Problems

Avoiding problems is also a tricky coping mechanism. Whether it's procrastination, living in the past, oversleeping, being excessively positive, or overworking, these methods might help you avoid thinking about stress temporarily, but they only let issues fester beneath the surface. Facing and addressing your emotions and problems, though tough, is important for managing stress effectively.

Spending Sprees

You know that rush you get when you buy something new? It feels great, right? But if you find yourself reaching for your credit card every time you feel stressed, it might be time to hit the pause button. Overspending can snowball into a serious problem, causing a ton of financial stress and even hurting your relationships. It's like trading one kind of stress for another.

Relying on Substances

Using something to escape stress can be tempting, but it's like trying to put out a fire with gasoline. You might feel good for a minute, but in the long run, you're just making things worse, and it is strictly not advised, no matter how good you think it is for you. If you find yourself relying on substances to cope, it's time to find some healthier ways to deal with your feelings.

Too Much Worry

It's smart to think about what might happen and consider the good and bad of a situation. But when worry starts taking over and stopping you from living your life, it's time to hit the brakes. You know, that feeling when you're convinced the worst is going to happen, even though there's no real reason to think that? Yeah, that's not helpful. Worry can actually make things feel worse, not better.

There are tons of ways people try to cope with life's challenges, but sometimes, those ways can do more harm than good. The first step is to realize when you're doing it. Just like finding a puzzle piece, once you see how something fits together, you can start to build a better picture. Changing habits takes time, but it's totally possible to find healthier ways to deal with life's ups and downs.

Negative Impacts of Anger

Anger isn't just an unpleasant emotion; lingering in anger for too long can seriously blow your health. When anger becomes too frequent, results in outlash or adverse reactions, is too intense, lasts too long, or is disproportionate to the triggering event, it can start to negatively affect your well-being. Let's explore some of the harmful impacts that anger can have.

Stress

Have you ever considered how stress plays into anger? Many people believe that stress is more common today than it was 20 years ago, and they also notice more anger in general.

Stress can definitely lead to a range of problems. If you're someone who tends to get angry easily, stress is likely to make those angry reactions more frequent and intense.

On the other hand, not all stress is bad. Healthy stress, or eustress, is what motivates us to get up in the morning and stay focused throughout the day. This kind of stress doesn't usually lead to anger or irritability. In fact, people who lack sufficient stress might be seen as "lazy" or "unmotivated" because they don't have enough drive to tackle their daily tasks.

On the other hand, distress is a type of stress that can lead to irritability and anger. It happens when stress becomes overwhelming and stops being a motivating force. You can think of this as stressors piling up one after another until it reaches a point where you can't manage them anymore, which results in an outburst of anger.

The link between stress and anger is deeply connected to both our psychological and physiological responses to perceived threats or challenges. To understand why stress often turns into anger, we need to look at how stress affects our thinking, emotional regulation, and our body's stress response system.

When we're stressed, our cognitive processing and perception change, making us more likely to see situations as threatening or frustrating. Stress can impair the function of the prefrontal cortex, which is the part of the brain that is responsible for decision-making and impulse control. As a result, we might have less patience and become more prone to anger over minor annoyances or setbacks.

Anger and stress can also start a vicious cycle that feeds on itself. Anger is a reaction to stress, and if anger is not controlled, it can lead to further stress. This feedback loop can become more severe. This cycle can be especially harmful because it can eventually raise stress and anger levels booth, which worsens the effects on one's physical and mental well-being.

Excessive Anger is Bad for Your Mental Health

Too much anger can seriously impact your mental health. Research indicates that emotional problems like depression and anxiety are frequently accompanied by increased anger,[3] which is linked to worsening symptoms and a reduced response to treatment.

According to APA, anger - especially sustained anger - can also have an impact on our ability to focus and think

---

[3] Sahu, A., Gupta, P., & Chatterjee, B. (2014). Depression is more than just sadness: a case of excessive anger and its management in depression. *Indian journal of psychological medicine, 36*(1), 77-79.

clearly. It may increase our hostility or cynicism, which may harm our capacity to create ties and form relationships. Our well-being may be harmed by all of this.

Our most significant relationships may suffer as a result of our angry outbursts. Because we are social beings, humans require social relationships. Violent or nasty verbal outbursts or even violent behavior can be triggered by anger.

Weakened Immune System

It has been noted that our emotional state of being partially reflects the condition of our immune system. Both levels of tension and relaxation are recognized by the immune system and taken into account when interpreting cues that trigger an immunological response. The way we perceive pain, experience inflammation, and find relief from pain is closely linked to our emotions and stress response. Anger can negatively impact the immune system, much like stress does. It can suppress immune cells, increase inflammation, and disrupt the balance of the immune response, leading to various health issues. These factors are linked to the emergence of inflammatory and autoimmune illnesses as well as the potential to increase an individual's susceptibility to infections.

Anger Causes Heart Stress

Anger can seriously impact heart health by triggering

the release of stress hormones. When you get angry, your body responds by releasing these hormones, which, over time, can put extra strain on your heart. This strain can weaken your heart's ability to pump blood effectively. As a result, you might experience high blood pressure and be at higher risk for serious conditions like heart disease, heart attacks, strokes, and metabolic syndrome.

Research shows that even brief moments of anger, visible through facial expressions, can affect heart function.[4] People who often feel angry - especially those who see the world as hostile and have trouble controlling their anger - are at a greater risk for coronary heart disease. Managing anger is important for maintaining heart health and reducing these risks.

Another study suggested that people with higher levels of trait anger face a greater risk of coronary heart disease.[5] Additionally, there is strong evidence linking anger directly to

---

[4] Rosenberg, E. L., Ekman, P., Jiang, W., Babyak, M., Coleman, R. E., Hanson, M., ... & Blumenthal, J. A. (2001). Linkages between facial expressions of anger and transient myocardial ischemia in men with coronary artery disease. *Emotion, 1*(2), 107.

[5] Sadeghi, B., Mashalchi, H., Eghbali, S., Jamshidi, M., Golmohammadi, M., & Mahvar, T. (2020). The relationship between hostility and anger with coronary heart disease in patients. *Journal of education and health promotion, 9*(1), 223.

an increased risk of heart attacks.

A systematic review, which analyzed data from nearly four thousand participants across over fifty medical centers in the United States, found that heart attacks are more than twice as likely to occur within two hours following an anger outburst. The study also noted that this risk increases with the intensity of the anger. In other words, the more intense the anger, the greater the risk to your heart, according to the researchers.[6]

Sleep Disturbances Due to Anger

Anger can seriously disrupt your sleep, and there are a few reasons why this happens. People who are more prone to anger often struggle with sleep because they tend to dwell on provocations and respond with anger. This can make it harder for them to manage their emotions and calm down before bed.

Research shows that people who have trouble controlling their anger or experience frequent anger are more likely to suffer from poor sleep. For instance, one study focused on middle-aged Korean men and women found that higher levels of anger were linked to significant increases in

---

[6] Mostofsky, E., Penner, E. A., & Mittleman, M. A. (2014). Outbursts of anger as a trigger of acute cardiovascular events: a systematic review and meta-analysis. *European heart journal, 35*(21), 1404-1410.

sleep disturbances, such as trouble falling and staying asleep.[7] Specifically, moderate to high anger levels were associated with a 40 to 70 percent higher risk of these sleep problems.

Additionally, anger can increase psychological arousal and mental unrest, which further complicates falling asleep. When your mind is racing with anger, it becomes even more tough to relax and get a good night's rest.

Impaired Cognitive Functioning and Anger

Impaired cognitive functioning refers to difficulties with thinking, memory, language, or judgment. When this intersects with anger, it can create a difficult situation. When it's tricky to think clearly, it can be easier to feel angry. You might have trouble understanding your own feelings or what others are going through. It can be hard to figure out how to handle a tough situation, which can make you feel frustrated and upset. You might forget things or have trouble finding the right words to say, which can also lead to anger.

Memory issues get in the way of learning from past mistakes, while communication problems can make anger

---

[7] Shin, C., Kim, J., Yi, H., Lee, H., Lee, J., & Shin, K. (2005). Relationship between trait-anger and sleep disturbances in middle-aged men and women. *Journal of Psychosomatic Research, 58*(2), 183-189.

stronger due to misunderstandings. Reduced impulse control can result in impulsive and harmful behaviors.

On the other hand, anger can negatively impact cognitive functioning. High stress levels due to anger can impair memory and concentration. Anger-related sleep disturbances also play a role in worsening cognitive difficulties. In addition, chronic anger can throw in physical health problems, which can also have an effect on cognitive abilities.

It's completely normal to feel angry when you're going through a tough time. Having firsthand experience with this emotion, I can understand. Even though it's okay to feel upset, it's really helpful to learn how to manage your anger. Doing this can help you feel better and heal in a healthy way. In the next chapter, we'll talk about some strategies to help you deal with anger.

Chapter 6: Strategies for Managing Anger During Grief

When I talk about anger, I remember the time when I was going through the grieving process and couldn't really figure out what was going on with my emotions, my mind, my heart, or simply the world around me. As I stated earlier, it was a mixed bag of emotions.

However, as I began my journey toward understanding my feelings, I came to the startling realization that I had been angry for an extended period of time. I had suppressed and ignored my anger because I believed it to be an 'unacceptable' feeling. Taking ownership of my anger allowed me to get hold of my sentiments.

Anger begins to seem like an okay response when you take into account the fact that it is frequently a reaction to mental or physical suffering as well as potential secondary emotions like depression, sorrow, grief, fear, etc.; what is not okay is to let it control you. Unlike depression, anger is characterized by a high level of energy - your body heats up, your pulse quickens, and you desire to do anything without giving it much thought. When this energy is channeled in a positive way, good things can happen. The issues we identify with rage are the result of unchecked, uncontrolled fury energy. We discuss handling, letting go of, and controlling anger because of this reason.

In my opinion, though there are different levels of anger, there are essentially two types: the immediate, intense kind that makes you want to explode, yell, or hit something and is essentially a result of frustration; and the slower, longer-lasting kind that is a result of ongoing pain. Unrecognized and unspoken, this second kind of anger can become toxic, leading to relationship and health issues before building into rage. Anger of any type, even the slow-boil type, has the potential to be constructive as well as destructive.

So, how can we transform our anger into something constructive? Well, finding constructive coping mechanisms and channels is especially important when dealing with anger that arises during the grieving process. Let's look at some of these techniques that can assist with constructive anger management.

Writing or Journaling

Writing about your anger might assist you

in realizing that it can be a defensive mechanism and that you can use this energy to make positive changes in your life. Because of the upsetting event that made you grieve and become angry, you can identify it as a warning sign that some important need isn't being met.

One of the most efficient methods to manage your anger and take constructive action is to write about it. Writing about anger helps you understand it, express it, and learn from it. You work through the causes of your rage by writing. You have more power once you understand the source of your anger because you can consider your options and choose some other reaction to it. You can use your anger as a teaching tool and take proactive steps to keep yourself safe from more hurt or disappointment. In my experience, anger can be turned into an emotion that causes you to become aware of yourself and wake up to do better.

In the heat of the moment, it's hard to write, so I suggest waiting till you are able to sit still. Then, write about your anger while you're still feeling it. Here are some starter writing prompts to get you going.

- Write down every wish, bad idea, and harmful instinct to help you release your anger. Write about your fantasies; scribble all the names you'd like to call yourself (if you're angry at yourself) or any other person or circumstance. Cross lines on the page using a pencil if that's what you feel like about a certain statement. It's alright. You may always shred it after you're done, and nobody will ever see what you wrote. Write until the rage starts to flow from your fingers onto the piece of paper or maybe until you're worn out or, much better until you're able to chuckle a bit at yourself.

- Ask yourself for what reason are you angry? What occurred to cause you pain? Was it someone else's doing? Something beyond your control? Spend 10 minutes to free-write, starting with, "I'm angry because..."

- What does your anger reveal about your own history? What self-revelation does it disclose to you? Write about your anger in a dialogue. Find out why it happens and what constructive action it encourages you to undertake to improve your mood.

- List a few concrete actions you can take and explain how you plan to complete them. What needs to be done to safeguard yourself against feeling hurt once more, or how can you react in a different way? For instance, you might choose to spend multiple sessions writing about the initial incident, or you might choose to go to therapy if, after writing, you discover that your reaction was caused by something that happened a long time ago - in simple terms, the most recent behavior or incident merely triggered your anger rather than actually causing it. If you conclude that you must leave a dangerous situation, make a list of the steps you must follow.

- Spend ten minutes writing freely about every means by which your anger gives you the power to improve your life for the better, starting with, "My anger empowers me to …"

The takeaway is that although anger doesn't always have to be a bad, destructive feeling, it can be. You will be in control of what you do with your anger by processing and understanding it.

Physical Activity

Anger management exercises are a useful tool for controlling rage and avoiding harm. These methods function by first calming you down and then assisting you in making constructive progress. When you feel your anger is becoming out of control, try these anger management exercises to help you feel relaxed again:

Practice Breathing

You may notice that your breathing becomes shallower and faster when you're upset. Breathing more slowly and deeply is a simple technique to relax your body and lessen your anger. Try taking calm, deep breaths via your mouth and nose. Instead of breathing deeply from your chest, do so from your abdomen. Breaths can be repeated as needed.

Progressive Muscle Relaxation

Muscle tension is one more indicator of physical stress that you may experience during an emotional outburst. You might want to attempt a progressive muscle relaxation technique to help you relax. This encompasses tensing and relaxing each body muscle group one at a time, gradually. Think about moving from the top of your head to your toes or the other way around.

Imagine Yourself Feeling Calm

Picture a peaceful place that makes you feel relaxed. Find a quiet, comfortable spot, close your eyes, and let your mind wander there. Think about the little details - what does it smell like? What sounds do you hear? Focus on how calm and good you feel in that special place.

Know Your Triggers

People often get angry about the same things repeatedly. Take some time to figure out what sets you off. Once you know your triggers, try to avoid them or find ways to handle them better. For instance, rather than being upset with your child all the time for the clutter, you could choose to close the door to their room when they don't tidy it. If you become easily agitated by traffic, it can also mean taking public transit rather than driving yourself to work.

Pause and Listen

When you're in a heated fight, you may find yourself making spontaneous judgments and saying hurtful things. Instead, stop and listen. You can control your anger and respond more effectively to the situation by making an attempt to listen to the other person in the conversation before you react.

Before you respond, give it some thought. If you feel like you need to cool off before you continue the talk, tell them you need to take a step away.

Modify Your Perspective

Feeling angry can cause you to overestimate the severity of the situation. Replace your negative thoughts with more grounded ones to help you feel less angry. One method to do this is to think critically and refrain from using absolute terms like "never" or "always". Keeping a balanced perspective on the world and transforming your irate demands into requests are two more effective tactics.

Steer Clear of Repetitive Thoughts

Even after the issue has been settled, you can find yourself thinking about the same thing that offended you repeatedly. This is referred to as ruminating or dwelling. Dwelling prolongs anger and increases the likelihood of conflicts or other problems.

Make an effort to let go of the source of your resentment. Try to focus on the good aspects of the person or circumstance that offended you instead of the negative ones.

Work Up a Sweat

You might wish to work up a sweat to soothe your nerves because aerobic activity has been explicitly identified as a technique to lessen rage in both children[8] and adults.[9]

---

[8] Tkacz, J., Young-Hyman, D., Boyle, C. A., & Davis, C. L. (2008). Aerobic exercise program reduces anger expression among overweight children. *Pediatric exercise science*, *20*(4), 390-401.

[9] McIntyre, K. M., Puterman, E., Scodes, J. M., Choo, T. H., Choi, C. J., Pavlicova,

Reduced feelings of rage, despair, and anxiety have been linked to exercises like treadmill running and rowing.[10]

The next time you need to let go of frustration, you might want to attempt refocusing your attention. In particular, the following workouts assist you in focusing on different movement challenges in order to momentarily shift your attention away from the source of your anger.

Boxing: Boxing workouts make you focus on different punch and jab combinations. They work your whole body, help you burn calories, and build strength, especially in your upper body. Many boxing studios and gyms also offer apps for home workouts if you can't make it to the gym. If you want a more budget-friendly option, you can just buy boxing gloves and gear and use a boxing app on your smartphone.

Jumping Rope: Jumping rope is another intense workout that demands focus and concentration. It quickly raises your heart rate and burns calories fast. The best part is it needs very little equipment. You can get a simple rope for under $15-$20 or

---

M., & Sloan, R. P. (2020). The effects of aerobic training on subclinical negative affect: A randomized controlled trial. *Health Psychology*, *39*(4), 255.

[10] Pels, F., & Kleinert, J. (2016). Does exercise reduce aggressive feelings? An experiment examining the influence of movement type and social task conditions on testiness and anger reduction. *Perceptual and motor skills*, *122*(3), 971-987.

opt for a complete system like CrossRope, which comes with weighted ropes and app-based workouts. Your jump rope routine can include moves like the double foot jump, running step, high step, or double unders. These exercises help you focus on coordinating your feet, which can distract you from anger and keep you engaged.

Circuit Training: Circuit workouts are great because they keep you on the move. You go from one station to the next, working different parts of your body for short bursts of time, which helps you focus less on what's making you angry. At home, you can do a circuit with basic equipment like dumbbells, kettlebells, or resistance bands. If you prefer, you can even do a bodyweight circuit using just your own body to build strength and get a good workout.

Step Away From It

Walking has many health benefits, like improving your heart health and lowering the risk of chronic diseases such as type 2 diabetes.[11] It can also help with releasing anger.

One study found that even a short 10-minute walk can

---

[11] Omura, J. D., Ussery, E. N., Loustalot, F., Fulton, J. E., & Carlson, S. A. (2019). Peer Reviewed: Walking as an Opportunity for Cardiovascular Disease Prevention. *Preventing chronic disease, 16.*

reduce feelings of hostility and anger, though the effect wasn't very strong.[12] Another study showed that reaching 10,000 steps a day led to lower anger levels, as well as reduced anxiety, depression, fatigue, confusion, and overall mood distress in overweight participants who followed a 12-week walking program.[13]

Next time you're feeling frustrated or exhausted, consider going for a walk with a friend or on your own. Just make sure you have the right shoes and clothes to avoid blisters and handle the weather.

Moreover, hiking on challenging terrain like forests, deserts, or mountains is a fantastic way to reduce stress and anger. Research shows that being in nature can really benefit your body.[14]

---

[12] Edwards, M. K., & Loprinzi, P. D. (2018). Experimental effects of brief, single bouts of walking and meditation on mood profile in young adults. *Health promotion perspectives, 8*(3), 171.

[13] Yuenyongchaiwat, K. (2016). Effects of 10,000 steps a day on physical and mental health in overweight participants in a community setting: a preliminary study. *Brazilian journal of physical therapy, 20*, 367-373.

[14] Thompson Coon, J., Boddy, K., Stein, K., Whear, R., Barton, J., & Depledge, M. H. (2011). Does participating in physical activity in outdoor natural environments have a greater effect on physical and mental wellbeing than physical activity indoors? A systematic review. *Environmental science & technology, 45*(5), 1761-1772.

Know Your Body

Anger causes your body to get extremely aroused. There may be an increase in your body temperature, respiration rate, blood pressure, and heart rate. Certain stress hormones that elevate your body's alertness are also released by your body.

Observe how you feel physically when you're upset. Find out what signals of anger your body sends. You can leave the space or attempt a relaxation method the next time you sense these signs.

Laughing To Decompress

Humor and playfulness can help you defuse uncomfortable situations, put things in perspective, lighten the mood, and resolve conflicts. Try adding a little lighthearted comedy to a situation if you find yourself getting upset. It can help you make your point without upsetting the other person or making them feel uncomfortable.

It's important, though, to laugh with the other person rather than at them. Steer clear of sarcasm and mean humor. When in doubt, begin with sarcastic humor directed at yourself. Everyone loves to laugh softly at themselves when they make mistakes. We're all fallible and have flaws, after all.

So, if you've goofed up, instead of getting angry, try

making a joke about it. Even if the joke doesn't land perfectly, the only person you might offend is usually yourself. Using humor and play to ease tension can even turn a potential conflict into a chance for deeper connection and understanding.

Seeking Support

One of the effective ways to manage anger while grieving is by leaning on the support of loved ones. Instead of keeping your feelings bottled up, talk to a trusted friend or family member who can offer a fresh perspective. Sharing your emotions with people who care about you provides a crucial outlet for processing what happened.

Pick friends or family members who are empathetic and understanding. Share your feelings with those who listen without judging, and be honest about your emotions using "I" statements, like "I feel angry when..." It's okay to set limits on how much you share, especially if someone is not supportive. Also, let loved ones help with practical tasks, like chores or meals, and appreciate their companionship.

Remember that you might have a strong support network to help you get through this trying period if you give it a thought or start accepting help. Never be afraid to ask for help - either practical or emotional - or just to lend an ear.

Speaking your mind is acceptable as long as you do it in a responsible manner. Get the support of a reliable friend to hold you responsible for responding calmly. No problem is solved by outbursts, yet calm conversation can make you feel less stressed and angrier. It might also prevent issues in the future.

Therapy or Counseling

You might want to look into professional assistance if, even after putting these earlier anger management strategies into practice, your anger is still out of control or if you're injuring other people or running afoul of the law. Counseling or therapy may be used for this.

Therapy, whether it be online, in a group setting, or one-on-one, can be an effective approach to discover triggers and investigate the causes of your anger. It's important to accept loss on an emotional and intellectual level; this may entail processing anger. Anger that is unresolved and dominating might eventually serve as a defense against sentiments of positivity, however few they may be.

Also, counseling can help people process their anger and redefine their relationship with the person who has passed away by exploring their feelings and changing their perspective. It provides safe ways to express anger toward the deceased or the situation. Bereavement counselors tailor their support to each person's needs. For complicated grief, revisiting good memories of the deceased can help balance out negative feelings, make it easier to express anger in a healthy way, or make room for other emotions to come out. Counselors help to understand that anger doesn't mean you don't care, and they make sure that anger is resolved in a way that doesn't overshadow the positive feelings. If anger isn't properly addressed, it could make your situation worse.

These five counseling strategies for dealing with loss and grief show different ways to support you through a tragic loss:

Cognitive Behavioral Therapy (CBT)

This method helps you spot and change negative thought patterns that can make it harder to process your grief. Negative thoughts can affect your feelings and behavior. CBT techniques include changing those thoughts, focusing on specific behaviors, and creating a new perspective on the loss.

Acceptance and Commitment Therapy (ACT)

This approach helps you move past grief by embracing it mindfully rather than resisting it. ACT involves focusing on your core values, committing to actions that help you achieve your goals, and accepting difficult emotions without judgment.

It also encourages being more aware and present in your daily activities. Another key part of ACT is creating distance between yourself and your thoughts, known as cognitive defusion. Finally, it helps you develop an "observing self," which means viewing your thoughts and feelings from a more detached perspective.

Traumatic Grief Therapy

Traumatic grief happens after a sudden and unexpected loss, and it can lead to physical and mental effects like intrusive thoughts, sleep problems, anxiety, and loss of appetite. Therapy for traumatic grief focuses on creating a routine to help manage emotions and calm the nervous system. You'll be encouraged to express your feelings and understand that what you're going through is normal.

Complicated Grief Therapy

This type of grief often follows traumatic grief and involves an intense focus on the loss and a strong desire for the deceased person to return. The American Psychiatric Association recognized prolonged grief disorder (PGD) as an official diagnosis in 2021. People with PGD may feel extremely sad, lonely, angry, or numb and might experience a loss of identity. They may avoid reminders of the loss or struggle to accept it. Complicated grief therapy usually combines different approaches, like ACT and CBT, to help you work through memories of the deceased, develop healthier ways to remember them, and strengthen your coping skills.

Interpersonal Therapy

Instead of focusing on past issues, interpersonal therapy looks at your current situation and relationships. Originally developed to treat major depression, it's also been adapted for grief counseling. There are two main types of interpersonal therapy. One is Metacognitive Interpersonal Therapy (MIT), which helps you identify and express your emotions. The second is Dynamic Interpersonal Therapy (DIT), which uses psychodynamics and mentalization to help you understand your thoughts and emotions more clearly.

Practice Self-Care

When grieving and angry, it's critical to put your needs first. It's not selfish to take care of yourself; in fact, it's essential to your healing process. Reducing stress, elevating your mood, and building resilience can all be achieved by partaking in relaxing activities. These small acts of self-compassion can add up, whether it's taking a warm bath, doing a hobby, or just spending time in nature.

In Chapter 8, we will go into more detail about the value of self-care. For the time being, keep in mind that caring for yourself is a significant step toward healing and a potent act of self-love.

Chapter 7: When Does It Get Easier?

Grief touches all of us at some point in our lives. It's a universal experience… something that connects us all as human beings…an experience that reminds us of our common vulnerability. When we lose someone or something that matters to us, whether it's a loved one, a relationship, a dream, or even a sense of identity, grief steps in, and our world shifts in ways we might not have expected. We all might feel that ache in our hearts, that emptiness that comes with loss. But while grief is something we all share, it's also intensely personal.

No one's grief is quite like yours as, in my opinion, no two people grieve the same way. The way you experience your loss, the way your emotions come to mind, the memories that surface, and the things that bring you comfort - or don't - are all unique to you. Your grief is a reflection of your relationship with what you've lost, of who you are, and of the life you've lived.

Your grief is as distinct as your fingerprint. It's important to recognize that just because someone else may have gone through something similar, their journey isn't completely identical to yours. What worked for them may not work with you, and that's perfectly okay. I think this is because grief doesn't follow a set path. It's not a linear process with steps that everyone follows in the same order. It's more like a winding road full of unexpected turns, ups and downs, and moments where you feel like you're backtracking.

You might find that some days you feel like you're moving forward or simply (and finally) making a little progress, and then suddenly, something - a scent, a place, a thing - pulls you right back into the depths of your sorrow. Other days, you might feel a little lighter, as if a small piece of the heaviness has lifted. This ebb and flow is natural, and it's all part of your journey.

As we move forward in this chapter, I'll share some thoughts and suggestions that might help you go through your own grief. But remember, these are just that - suggestions. As I mentioned earlier, too, there's no 'one-size-fits-all' approach to grief. What's most important is that you acknowledge your own process, listen to your own needs, and give yourself the space and grace to grieve in the way that feels right for you. Having said that, this obviously doesn't include the harmful ways of grieving.

This is your journey. It's okay if it doesn't look like anyone else's. It's okay if it takes longer than you thought it would or if it feels different than you expected. Grief is a reflection of love, and just as love is unique, so too is the way we grieve.

You're not alone in this, even though it may sometimes feel that way. Grief connects us all, but it's your personal experience that makes your journey through it unlike anyone else's. And that's something worth accepting.

It's a Long Road

When you lose something or someone who was an important part of your life, like a child or a spouse, it can take years - often three to five - to start feeling a sense of renewal again in life. But in some ways, grief starts to feel a little more bearable after just some months.

The truth is, there's no real 'better' when it comes to grief. The person you loved is still gone, and that never changes. What happens is that we learn to live with their absence. Over time, we might find ourselves changing, growing into someone new just to find a way to reconnect with life, even as we carry the loss with us.

The pain does become more manageable, though. In my experience, the first few months are the toughest. I think this is because the pain is inexorable - there's no break from the heartache and sorrow, not even for a moment. After about six months, you might start to notice a few moments of calm, but the pain still overshadows everything. For some people, the second year might hit even harder than the first when the reality that they're never coming back truly sinks in. We usually pin our hopes on that first anniversary, as if it's a milestone that will somehow change things - as if our pain will suddenly fade or they'll somehow return. But when that day passes, and nothing is different, it can trigger another layer of extreme sadness.

As time passes, though, things begin to shift. The layers of intense pain start to come less often, and those moments of peace become more recurrent. But even years down the road, a sudden gush of heartache can hit you out of nowhere, making it feel like the loss is brand new all over again.

Grieving a major loss is like being in a boxing ring with an opponent who's gradually losing strength. After a year or two, the punches don't hurt as much, and you start to feel like you can handle it. As the hits come less frequently, you might even let your guard down. Sometimes, when a punch does land, you might even welcome it, as it reminds you of the reason you're still in the ring. But every now and then, a punch might come out of nowhere and knock you off your feet.

Some moments might catch you completely off guard just when you think you're doing okay. Maybe it's around the fourteen-month mark, and you're out for a peaceful walk, feeling all calm and steady. Then, out of nowhere, something as simple as the scent of lilacs might hit you like a ton of bricks.

You might remember how much your loved one adored lilacs and how you planted them together around your home. The year before they passed, those lilacs might have grown tall enough to create a private little space, and when they bloomed, the two of you would step outside just to breathe in that sweet scent.

You might have moved to a new place and never thought about those lilacs, maybe because it's somewhere like a desert, and supposed that you might never encounter lilacs again. You might not even know they could grow there. But one day, as you're walking, you catch that familiar scent drifting toward you from a vacant lot. And because you weren't braced for it, the memory might blindside you, leaving you reeling for days, maybe even weeks.

This was just an example of how unexpected the waves and layers of grieving can be and how unpredictable the timeline for the grieving cycle is for everyone. As is the common case, as the years go by, maybe four or so, those intense waves of grief might start to fade. When they do come, they might feel more like nostalgia for what you shared rather than the sharp pain of what you've lost.

Acknowledge Your Emotions

Grief is a messy, unpredictable thing. One minute, you might feel like you're holding it together, and the next, you're falling apart over something very simple. It's easy to wonder if what you're feeling is 'normal' or if you're grieving the 'right' way. Let me tell you - there is no 'correct' way to feel your emotions.

When I was in the thick of my grief, I felt like I was on an emotional rollercoaster that I hadn't signed up for. One moment, I'd be drowning in sadness, and the next, I'd feel this overwhelming anger or even a weird sense of relief. It was confusing, and I didn't always know what to do with those feelings. Maybe you've felt something similar.

But I feel like every emotion we experience during grief is a result of a sadness deep inside our hearts. Yes, even the ones that seem contradictory or that you're not 'supposed' to feel. It's okay to be angry, to feel guilty, to cry, or even to laugh unless it doesn't harm anyone or yourself. It's all part of the process.

Society loves to put us in boxes, telling us how we should act and how we should feel. When it comes to grief, though, those boxes don't apply. Grief isn't neat and tidy, and it definitely doesn't stick to a schedule. Some people cry a lot;

some don't cry at all. Some talk about their feelings openly, while others keep them close to their chest. However you grieve, that's your way.

If there's one thing I've learned, it's that suppressing your feelings doesn't make them go away - it just makes them louder later on. I tried to ignore my grief at times, thinking that if I just stayed busy, it wouldn't hurt so much. But all that did was push those emotions deeper until they came rushing back when I least expected it.

So, please, don't feel like you have to keep it all inside. Find a way to let it out, whether that's talking to someone you trust, writing about it, or even just taking a moment to really feel whatever it is you're feeling. It's okay to give yourself permission to grieve in your own way, at your own pace.

Routine And a Sense of Normalcy

Coming to terms with the death of a loved one can make the idea of getting back to daily life feel like something impossible. It might feel like their death takes everything you know, shatters it into a million pieces, and then scatters them everywhere. Suddenly, the routine you once had feels like it's in a million pieces, and it's hard to see how they'll ever fit together again.

It's completely normal to feel like your life is out of

sync after such a huge loss. Everything might seem disjointed, and it might feel like nothing will ever make sense again. But while this cataclysm is unquestionably tough, it also opens up a chance for you to rebuild and grow.

Building routines and structure can be healing when you're going through loss. Even though it might feel like the world is spinning out of control, organizing things in your daily life can bring you some comfort. Start by setting up a simple daily routine that gives you a sense of normalcy. Even small things, like eating meals at the same time each day or taking a short walk, can help you to bring a bit of stability.

Try to set small, easy-to-achieve goals for yourself. Completing simple tasks, like tidying up or drinking a glass of water, can also make a big difference. These small wins can help you feel more in control and boost your mood.

When I say try to set up a routine, I don't mean for you to dive right into it and get things set up within a day. I do not intend to tell you to rush through your grief. I just want you to start small and take the first step toward feeling normal again.

Setting Small Achievable Goals

While goal-setting is important at any stage of life, it can be especially beneficial after a loved one has passed away. Even though short-term goals might help you stay focused as you move closer to your longer-term objectives, long-term goals can give you something to work toward and give you hope during a trying moment.

You should always aim for achievable and reasonable goals. Sharing your objectives with someone else can also be beneficial since they can hold you responsible and provide you with the support and inspiration you need to keep going. Let's talk about some strategies for setting sensible objectives and finding comfort when grieving:

Examine Your Career Route

You may be considering the idea that life is too short to continue with unfulfilling responsibilities and hobbies while you mourn the loss of your loved one. This could be a great chance to make a change if you happen to be currently overworked or dissatisfied with your employment. Why not consider what other jobs you could carry out? Perhaps you could even launch your own business.

Starting a business is no small feat, but it can be rewarding. You'll need to do some groundwork, like conducting market research to make sure your idea is practical, choosing a name, writing a solid business plan, making a marketing strategy to get the word out, etc.

Get Involved in the Community

Isolation can be harmful to your health and well-being as well as the healing process. Try to establish connections with people in your neighborhood. One way to do this is by volunteering for a good cause like feeding the homeless through an organization. Helping others can bring a sense of purpose to your life and give you the chance to socialize and make new friends along the way. You may also join a book club or a gardening club with like-minded individuals.

Moreover, you can look into classes at a nearby institution if you want to pick up new skills and expertise. It's likely that you can enroll in a class that teaches you how to cook or learn a foreign language, which will allow you to continue being productive.

Put Pen To Paper

As discussed earlier, one of the ways to communicate your ideas and feelings is through writing. Think about keeping a notebook in which you can record your daily experiences, list your objectives, and go over the measures you plan to take to reach them.

Writing letters to your close friends and family members is an additional option. In these letters, you may share your story with them. Alternatively, you may pen a letter to yourself. When writing to yourself, don't be afraid to be frank and honest with yourself. Even if you don't share all you write, it can still be beneficial to your well-being.

Develop a Healthy Lifestyle

Have you ever noticed how much better you feel after a good night's sleep or a healthy and delicious meal? It's not just in your head. Taking care of your body is actually a powerful way to calm your mind and handle stress.

As you grieve, make an effort to eat a healthy diet. Regular meals fuel your body and brain. When you eat balanced meals, you provide your body with the energy it needs to function properly. This means you're less likely to feel cranky or overwhelmed. Plus, eating regularly helps to stabilize your blood sugar, which can have a big impact on your mood.

At the end of the day, improving your physical health through action will have a beneficial effect on your mental health. Pick a daily physical activity that gets your blood flowing, such as cycling, walking, jogging, playing sports, or anything else. Frequent exercise has a significant positive impact on your long-term health, energy level, and mood. It also helps in boosting your mood. When you move your body, it releases feel-good chemicals called endorphins. These endorphins can help in reducing your stress and anxiety.

Exercise also helps to improve your sleep quality, which, as we know, is important for managing stress.

Additionally, getting enough sleep is essential for overcoming sadness. Try setting up a nightly routine to help you unwind from the day and obtain the quality sleep you require if you suffer from insomnia. Moreover, sleep can be considered as a reset button type of phenomenon. When you get enough quality sleep, your body and mind have a chance to recharge. It's during sleep that your brain sorts through the day's events and processes information. Lack of sleep can make you feel irritable, anxious, and unable to concentrate. Create a bedtime routine and aim for 7-9 hours of sleep each night. This can make a big difference in how you feel and handle daily challenges.

While there is no one best way to grieve, everyone who has experienced a loss in their life can gain from making positive goals for themselves. Take a fresh look at your work and increase your community involvement. Initiate writing, and try to establish habits that help to keep you healthy and happy.

You Can Remember Them!

Remembering someone or something we've lost can be a soothing part of the healing process. You can remember your loved ones in a lot of ways. Let's discuss a few of them.

One simple way is to create a memory book. This can be a personal project where you collect photos, letters, and little keepsakes that remind you of them. You can add your own notes, stories, and memories, which can turn the book into a special keepsake. This could also turn into something that you could revisit to go through fond memories. Another way to remember your loved one is by talking about them in a gathering with family and friends. You can share their stories, talk about them, or simply make their favorite food.

Who knows, doing these things might make you feel just a little better. I know this because even the simplest tasks can feel devastating when you're grieving. Things you once did without a second thought, like making a cup of coffee or taking a shower, might suddenly seem like insurmountable challenges. It's as if your energy reserves are depleted, and every little thing requires a tremendous effort. That's why setting small, achievable goals daily is important while you're grieving.

The important thing to remember and extract from all we have discussed is that you're not in a race to overcome your pain. I have said it before, and I'll say it again: grief is a journey without a set timeline. Everyone experiences it differently, and it's okay to take the time you need. Be gentle with yourself, and understand that it's normal to have ups and downs along the way. As long as you do not hurt others, allow yourself to feel your emotions. Even if you get sudden outbursts of anger at other people but realize it later, simply apologize. There is no shame in acknowledging your mistake and simply asking for forgiveness. I strongly believe that it takes great courage to apologize. I think only brave people can truly feel sorry for their slip-ups and actually apologize. So, even if you hurt someone along the way, try to think about the whole situation, understand your stance but their point of view as well, and then, simply discuss it with them and apologize.

Having said that, be patient with yourself and show yourself some self-compassion as you move through this process. Remember, it's not about rushing to 'get over' your grief but rather about finding a way to live with it in a healthy manner as part of your ongoing story. You've got this!

Chapter 8: It's Okay To Be Happy Again

Fear. It's this sneaky little chum that seems to follow grief around like an awkward friend you didn't invite to the party but can't seem to shake off. If you're anything like me, you've probably noticed its quiet presence in the background. We've already talked about this. It's normal. Fear shows up in strange places during grief.

Maybe it's the fear of forgetting, the fear of moving on, or even the fear of being okay again. Whatever shape it takes, it's not something to wrestle with or defeat, but more like a guest that eventually finds its way out once it's overstayed its welcome.

And while fear hangs around, there's something we often forget to bring to the table: self-care. It's easy to neglect ourselves when we're just trying to get through the day, but the truth is, taking care of yourself is like giving grief a little more space to breathe without suffocating your joy.

When a typical person thinks about self-care, they might imagine bubble baths or a good night's sleep (though, who doesn't love those?). But it's actually not limited to these things. Self-care, in my opinion, is more about finding those tiny moments that bring you peace, even in the chaos. It can be simply about enjoying a cup of tea, taking a quiet walk, or just sitting with your thoughts without judgment. Practically anything that makes you feel like yourself again.

It's no new news that grief is exhausting! But tending to your own comfort along the way might help you keep going.

And honestly, the thing to keep in mind here is that self-care is *not* selfish. It's easy to feel guilty for taking time to focus on yourself when you're grieving, but let's set the record straight. Self-care is important for your mental, emotional, and physical health, especially during times like these.

Grief takes a toll, and without pausing to nurture yourself, you run the risk of running on empty. Here, I want you to think of self-care as refueling - taking that extra moment to care for your needs allows you to process emotions more clearly, find balance, and ultimately heal. Whether it's resting, talking to a friend, or just stepping back for some quiet time, these moments aren't indulgent - they're vital.

You can't pour from an empty cup, right? Taking care of yourself helps you better show up in life, for others, and, more importantly, for *you*.

Make Self-Care A Priority

Now, let's take this up a notch. When I say self-care is important, I do not mean it as a suggestion or something to do 'if you have time.' It should be a part of your daily routine in order to help you stay mentally, emotionally, and physically healthy, especially when you're grieving. Grief demands so much from us, and without some form of self-care in place, we risk becoming astounded, exhausted, and disconnected from ourselves and, in some cases, others as well.

You can consider self-care like maintenance for your well-being. You wouldn't drive your car on an empty tank, right? In the same way, you can't expect to overcome grief - something so heavy and emotionally draining - without refueling yourself regularly. This is where scheduling comes in. It might sound odd at first, but having a routine where self-care is prioritized can make a big difference.

Make it a part of your daily life. Seriously, put it in your calendar, set reminders on your phone, whatever it takes to commit to it. It can be a 10-minute break to step outside, a cup of tea with no distractions, or an hour-long conversation with your best friend. Just find what works for you and *stick to it*.

And don't let guilt creep in. As I said earlier, it's not selfish to take this time for yourself. In fact, it's necessary.

You're nurturing yourself so you can show up more fully for the people you love, your responsibilities, and, more importantly, *your own healing.*

One of the practical ways to start is to breathe - really breathe! We have a habit of holding our breath or breathing shallowly when we're stressed, anxious, or grieving. However, the act of consciously taking deep breaths is one of the simplest forms of self-care. We discussed this earlier, too, but let's have a look at it again.

Start by closing your eyes (if it feels right), take a deep breath in through your nose, hold it for a few seconds, and then exhale slowly through your mouth. Feel the tension melt away with every exhale. Do this a few times throughout the day - it's a quick reset button for your mind and body. Sometimes, it's the small, simple acts of care that make the biggest difference.

If you're new to scheduling self-care, you can also try to pick one or two activities you enjoy and make them part of your daily routine for the next week. These can be as simple as taking a walk in your nearby park or reading a book. The key is consistency. By setting a routine soon enough, you'll notice how much better equipped you are to handle not only grief but the ups and downs of life.

At first, it may feel like another 'task' added to your to-do list, but trust me, it's one worth keeping. Over time, it transforms from a task into a practice that gives you energy and peace, especially during those dark moments. The more you practice self-care, the more you realize it's not an escape from grief but a way to steer through it with grace and strength.

Setting Boundaries

Boundaries… yes… in my opinion, these are the invisible lines we all need to keep our sanity intact. Setting boundaries might sound like a big, serious thing, but it's really just about knowing what works for you and what doesn't.

First things first: be honest with yourself. Ask yourself these questions:

Does being around people recharge your batteries or run them down?

If you're someone who likes social interaction, then fine. But if being around a crowd feels more like an energy drain, it's okay to recognize that, too.

What activities do you enjoy with friends, and which ones feel like you're running a marathon?

It's fine to love a good game night but loathe planning it. Knowing what energizes you and what feels like a chore can help you make better choices about how you spend your time.

Are you good at saying what you need?

Sometimes, we hope people will just magically understand our limits. Spoiler alert: they won't. It's perfectly okay to be clear about what you need and how you can best be supported.

If you're not sure where you stand with your boundaries, ask a few close friends or family members. They might shed some light on whether you're the one in the wrong or if you're balancing things just right. Just basically get an objective point of view from a third person because we might think we're doing things right when we're actually not and are just being toxic or just over-pleasing, ultimately hurting ourselves or others in the process.

Now comes the part that many people dread to do: learning to say no. It might feel a little strange at first, but saying no to things that don't serve you is just as important as saying yes to things that do.

You can think of it this way. Your time and energy are like a limited-edition cake. You wouldn't give slices away to just anyone, would you? Save those slices for the activities and people that really bring you comfort or joy. It's okay to skip out on some things that are actually harmful to you. So, set some boundaries and stick by them.

Start Small

If you started a new hobby, you wouldn't jump into the deep end of a pool without testing the waters first, correct? The same goes for finding what self-care practices work best for you.

Self-care can take on many forms, from the subtle to the more prominent. You might start by infusing your space with elements that make you feel good, like surrounding yourself with colors and scents that uplift your mood. Maybe it's a soothing lavender candle or a cozy, colorful blanket. These background touches can make a big difference in how you feel day to day.

On the other hand, you can start with a few tiny self-care activities. This could be setting aside a specific amount of time each day for an activity that you find restorative, like reading, writing, journaling, or knitting. The idea is to create a little oasis in your schedule where you can focus on yourself.

Start small. Introduce just one new self-care practice at a time. This can help make it easier to build a habit without feeling overwhelmed. Maybe you begin by adding five minutes of quiet time to your morning routine or placing a small, relaxing plant on your desk. As these small practices become a natural part of your day, you can gradually add more if you like.

One important thing to remember here is to find activities that really resonate with you. Self-care is deeply personal, so what works wonders for one person might not be your cup of tea (literally or figuratively). The goal is to discover what makes you feel good and stick with it. You might need to try a few things to see what brings you the most comfort and happiness. So, keep it playful, keep it personal, and, more importantly, enjoy the journey of discovering what works best for you.

Be Kind and Gentle with Yourself

I know your journey with grief is tough. I know you think nobody knows how you feel. I understand you might have thoughts... dark thoughts about yourself, the situation, or others. I know... I've been there.

Still, I would say that during this time, one of the most important things you can do for yourself is to be kind and gentle throughout the process. I'm not asking you to practice self-care to achieve perfection or have everything together. I'm asking you to do so so that you give yourself the time and understanding you need to heal.

I would like you to use this self-care tool as a way to extend kindness to yourself. Just wrap yourself in a cozy blanket of compassion. You don't have to get everything right or follow a strict regimen. Instead, focus on allowing yourself the grace to feel what you need to feel and taking small steps toward comfort and healing.

Sometimes, showing others kindness makes us feel good about ourselves. Here are some ideas that you can do to sprinkle kindness into your day:

- You can take a plate of cookies to your neighbors. Who doesn't love cookies? It's a sweet way to show you care and maybe even make a new friend.

- You can hold the elevator if you see someone rushing.

- Similarly, you can hold the door for someone – it's simple but effective.

- Pay for someone's coffee. Next time you're in line at the coffee shop, you can pay for the person behind you. It's a lovely surprise that can set their day off right.

- While you're out for a walk, pick up any litter you see.

- Ask someone how they are, and really listen. Showing genuine interest in someone's well-being can mean a lot.

- You can try to offset your carbon footprint and contribute to the planet's health with a tree-planting effort.

- You can reach out to someone struggling. Let them know you're there for them.

- Send five texts. Let five people know how important they are to you. A simple message can make a big impact.

- Forgive someone. Letting go of grudges can be a powerful act of kindness for both you and the other person.

- You can also bring breakfast to work - share bagels or other treats with your colleagues. It's a nice way to start the day on a positive note.

These small acts of kindness are not just going to impact others - they're going to impact you as well. They can bring a sense of fulfillment and joy, which can help in making your self-care journey a bit brighter. Give them a try and see how a little kindness can go a long way!

Your Support System

Let's talk about your support system. Normally, these are the people you lean on and trust. Sometimes, we need a little nudge from those around us to remember why self-care matters and to keep us accountable.

Reaching out to loved ones can be incredibly helpful in prioritizing your self-care. They can remind you of the importance of taking time for yourself and offer gentle encouragement when you're struggling. Plus, having someone check in on you can make it easier to stick to those self-care practices you're trying to build into your routine.

Ask yourself these questions to get a clearer picture of your support system:

Who do I trust and lean on?

Are you making sure they know they're an important part of your circle? Sometimes, we assume people know their role in our lives without saying it out loud. A little acknowledgment can go a long way in strengthening those bonds.

Do I need to expand my circle?

Are there people who want to be part of your support network but aren't yet included for reasons that might not be valid? It could be worth reconsidering if adding more people could offer you additional support.

Are there people in my circle who shouldn't be there?

Maybe there are people whose presence doesn't align with your comfort. It's okay to reassess and make changes to make sure your support system is actually supportive.

Engage with those you trust and let them know how

they can help. They might offer to check in with you regularly, join you for self-care activities, or simply be there to listen. The key is to communicate openly and make sure your support network is set up to nurture and uplift you.

If you think about it for a moment, building a strong support system can change the self-care journey from a solo mission into a whole experience, which might make it easier for you to stay committed and feel less alone. So, don't hesitate to ask for help within your circle and keep them in the loop. Sometimes, a little support is all you need to turn self-care into a natural and rewarding part of your life.

As we wrap up this chapter, let's take a moment to remember something important: it's okay to seek happiness and keep moving forward while still remembering your loved one. Grief is a journey that can feel overwhelming at times, but it doesn't mean you have to put your life on hold or wait until you're feeling 'better' to enjoy life again.

Finding a balance is key. In my opinion, moderation in every aspect of life is very important. Life doesn't have to be all or nothing; you can have both. You can smile and find happiness, all while remembering your loved one.

You can think of it this way. Your loved one is a part

of your story, but they don't have to be the only part. You can keep their memory close to your heart and still absorb the beautiful moments life has to offer. Enjoy the small joys, like a warm cup of coffee or a kind gesture from a friend.

So, as you go through your days, keep in mind that it's fine to blend the past with the present. Your loved one can be with you in your heart, and you can still make room for new experiences and happiness.

The journey forward can be full of light, love, and even laughter. Accept what had happened, and know that it's okay to move forward while still holding your loved one close to your heart. In the end, my dear, it's okay to be happy again!

Chapter 9: The New Normal

When we think of resilience, we usually imagine someone who bounces back quickly from a tough situation, like a rubber band snapping back into shape. But when it comes to grief, resilience looks a little different. It's not about bouncing back; it's about finding a way to keep going, even when life feels completely upside down.

Resilience is about growing through the pain. It's like learning to live with a new normal, one where things might not ever be the same, but that doesn't mean they can't be okay again. When I say 'resilient,' I don't mean forgetting or 'getting over' the loss. As an alternative, I mean for you to figure out how to carry the love and memories with you as you continue moving forward at your own pace.

I think resilience isn't a superpower… it's more like a part of being human. In my opinion, we all have it within us, even when we don't feel particularly strong. And while grief changes us, it also opens up the possibility of discovering a deeper strength and compassion we might not have known we had.

There are ways to grieve while being resilient. Let's have a look at some:

Focus Your Attention

Our brains can only handle so much at once, right? That's why it's super important to be mindful of what we focus on, especially when we're grieving. Take blaming, for example. It's one of those things that feels like it might get us somewhere but usually just ends up draining our energy. Instead, we can choose to pay attention to things that actually help us conserve our emotional energy.

You can think of it like this: you're already going through a lot, so why scatter your energy even more? Instead, try focusing on things that fill your tank, like sticking to daily routines, nurturing your relationships, or practicing self-care. These small actions add up over time and help keep you grounded, even when everything else feels a bit out of control.

Acknowledging What You Can Change (and What You Can't)

I have been there with the 'what ifs.' You might have gone through or might be going through them presently. They just keep coming, and honestly, I know they can be very exhausting. It's totally normal to have those thoughts, but the trick is not to let them run the show. Like, yes, it's okay to acknowledge them but don't let them take over your mental energy.

Dr. Rick Hanson, a psychologist and Senior Fellow of UC Berkeley's Greater Good Science Center, has this analogy: he says the mind is like Velcro for the bad stuff and Teflon for the good stuff. Resilient grieving helps you flip that script a little bit. It gives you the tools to step out of that constant fight-or-flight mode and instead notice what's safe and comforting around you.

Searching for Optimistic Emotions

One thing resilient people tend to do is make room for positive feelings. And it's not just because they feel good - it's because they actually do good! Optimistic sentiments can rewire our brains and help us see the world in a brighter light. Now, I get it - when you're grieving, it's not always easy to think positively all the time. But you don't have to force it. Instead, try creating good experiences, even in small ways. It could be as simple as helping someone out, like giving directions to a stranger. Little things like that can spark a chain reaction of good feelings that carry you through tough moments.

Accepting the Good

Psychologists might call this 'benefit finding,' but in

real life, it's just about accepting the good things when they come your way. Maybe it's like simply letting your family or friends support you or not beating yourself up if you find yourself enjoying something, even while in the process of grieving.

Resilience while grieving helps you find a balance between your sadness and your future. It's not about ignoring your loss but learning to live with it while also allowing yourself to feel relaxed when you feel like it. Going back and forth between those emotions is a natural part of the healing process. And when you let the good in, it can recharge your emotional batteries and help you face the harder days with a bit more strength.

Hope

At some point, you might have experienced moments when you might have felt that hope was out of reach. Things don't always go the way we want, but hope can be one of the most powerful tools for healing, especially when it comes to mental health.

Wishing for a better outcome isn't the only thing that hope entails. It gives people who are struggling a sense of purpose and motivation and helps them push through the tough times and face the challenges life throws their way.

Hope is basically believing that something good can happen. It's about trusting that things will improve. We might hope for something as small as a traffic-free commute or something like our favorite team winning the championship. When we apply hope to the grieving process, I think it can make a huge difference. People who hold onto hope usually see better outcomes.

Building hope while dealing with a loss isn't always a breeze, but it's definitely possible with the right support and tools. One of the best ways is by staying connected. Whether it's through therapy, joining support groups, or leaning on friends and family, having people in your corner can really make a difference.

Another thing that helps is setting small, manageable goals, as we discussed earlier. Even little wins can make you feel like you're moving forward. Doing things that make you happy, taking care of yourself, and trying to live as healthy as you can also do wonders for your mood.

It's also important to challenge those negative thoughts that pop up. Using techniques like cognitive-behavioral therapy can help you reframe those thoughts in a more positive and realistic way. And, of course, if you need extra guidance, talking to a therapist or counselor who knows their stuff can be very helpful - they can create a plan just for you.

Hope is a really powerful tool when it comes to overcoming mental health issues like depression, anxiety, addiction, or trauma. It gives you the strength to keep going, even when things get tough. People who focus on hope usually see better results and generally feel better about their lives.

Life After Loss

As you move through grief, you start hearing a phrase that pops up a lot: 'the new normal.' At first, it can feel a little strange - like, what does that even mean? Well, the new normal is basically life after the loss. It's the way things shift and settle into something different, even if it's not what you expected.

But the thing is that life after loss does *change*. It doesn't snap back to exactly how it was before, and honestly, that's okay. The new normal is about adjusting to these changes, even if they're not what you expected. You can find your way in a life that looks a little (or a lot) different.

It's okay if you don't overcome the feelings of grief after the loss quickly. The love… the memories… they stick with you. But over time, life begins to evolve in ways that are unique to you. You start to find your new routines, new moments of joy, and maybe even a fresh perspective…

And while this new normal might not feel *normal* at first, it might become part of your journey.

I'm not telling you to pretend that everything is fine or 'moving on' like the loss never happened. The truth is, you're not leaving anything behind. You're carrying it all with you, but you're also making space for new experiences and for hope to slowly re-enter your world.

Everyone's version of the new normal looks different. There's no one-size-fits-all. It's more about figuring out what feels right for you. Some days, it might feel like you're making progress, and other days, it might feel like you're stuck. And that's okay! Healing isn't a straight line but more like a winding path with a few twists and turns along the way.

The beauty of this new normal is that it can still be full of meaning, growth, and, yes, even comfort. Life evolves, and so do you, as you learn to live with the loss while also embracing everything that's still ahead. So, be patient with yourself as you find your footing, and remember that while things might be different, they can still be beautiful in a new and unexpected way.

Allowing Yourself to Thrive in the New Normal

So, as your life shifts and this 'new normal' starts to take shape, one of the most important things is learning to accept it. And let's be real - acceptance doesn't mean you have to love everything about the changes. It's more about acknowledging that life *has* changed and finding a way to live in this new reality.

Acceptance doesn't happen overnight. It's more like a slow unfolding, and that's okay. It's about understanding that, while things aren't what they used to be, you still have the power to shape how you move forward. Life after loss is a blend of holding on to the past and making room for the future, and that balance takes time.

Once you begin to accept this new reality, it opens the door for growth. You're not stuck in the past or wishing things could go back to how they were. Instead, you're choosing to adapt. And adapting doesn't mean forgetting or moving on in a way that erases your grief. It just means finding new ways to thrive within this changed landscape.

This can look different for everyone. Maybe it's creating new hobbies that bring you joy. Maybe it's reconnecting with friends or discovering something about yourself that you didn't even realize was there before. It's all about taking those small steps that help you feel more grounded in your new normal.

The key is giving yourself permission to thrive, even if it feels a little strange at first. It's okay to find happiness again. It's okay to smile, to make plans, and to feel hope creeping back in. I don't mean to say that you'll be free of grief when you thrive in this new normal, but more like you'll probably learn how to live comfortably alongside it.

By accepting your reality and adapting, you might open yourself up to growth, resilience, and, yes, even some relaxation. You might be surprised by how much strength you discover along the way and how life, though different, can still hold so much for you.

Healing Together

When you've gone through something as life-changing as grief, you come out the other side with a deep understanding of what that pain feels like. And while it's not a journey you'd wish on anyone, there's something about using your own experience to support others who are going through it, too. It's like you've been given this unique insight into grief, and now you have the ability to offer empathy and understanding that only someone who's walked that path can.

Supporting others doesn't have to be anything grand or overwhelming. You could simply offer someone a listening ear, share a comforting word, or just sit quietly with someone as they process their own loss. Sometimes, it's those small gestures of kindness that make a huge difference.

If you look at it in a different way, you might notice

that by reaching out and supporting others, you're not only helping them - you're also helping yourself. There's a healing power in knowing that your pain and your journey can bring comfort to someone else. It can create a sense of connection that makes the weight of grief feel just a little bit lighter.

And let's not forget about the sense of community that comes from sharing these experiences. When we support each other, we create a bond that reminds us we're not alone. Grief can make us feel isolated but by offering and accepting support, we're able to build connections that can help carry us through the toughest days. There's something healing in knowing that we're in this together, that we don't have to face our struggles alone.

Grief changes us, no doubt. While grief may always be a part of your story, it doesn't have to define your future. Life after a loss might never be exactly the same, but that doesn't mean it can't have growth and comfort in it. There will be moments when the sadness feels heavy, and that's okay - it's part of the journey. But there will also be moments of light, where hope begins to flicker again, and you find yourself smiling, dreaming, and hoping for the best for the future.

So, take a deep breath, trust the process, and stay positive that brighter days might just be ahead. With time, patience, and compassion for yourself and others, you might discover that hope is just on the horizon.